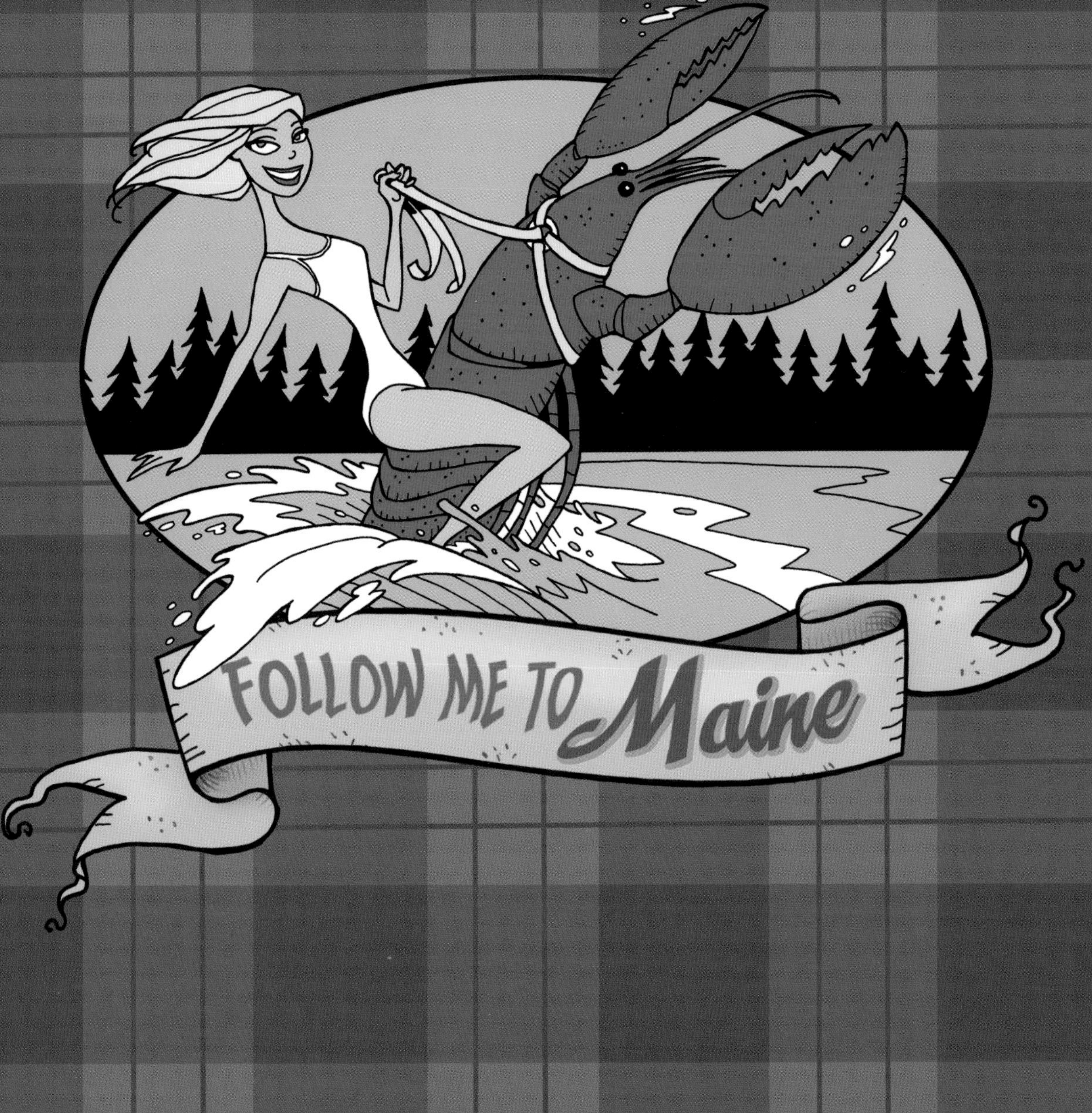
FOLLOW ME TO Maine

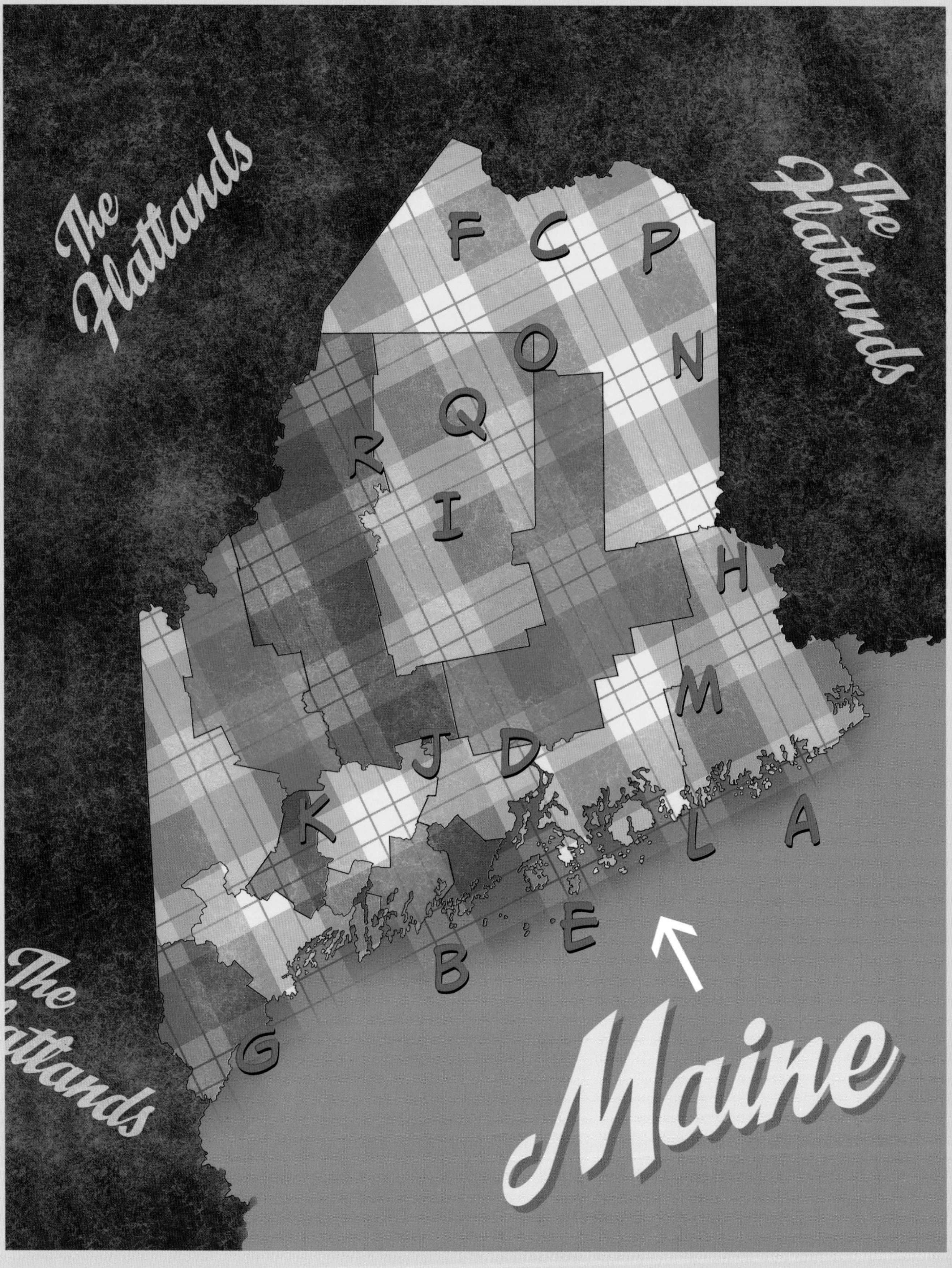

The Flatlands
The Flatlands
The Flatlands
F
C
P
O
N
Q
R
I
H
M
J
D
K
L
A
E
B
G
Maine

THE LEGEND OF Maine

MATCH THE LEGEND ITEM TO ITS LOCATION ON THE MAP:

☐

☐

☐

☐

☐

☐

☐

☐

☐

☐

☐

☐

☐

☐

☐

☐

☐

☐

ISLANDPORT PRESS

Islandport Press
P.O. Box 10
Yarmouth, Maine 04096

books@islandportpress.com
www.islandportpress.com

ISBN: 978-1-934031-49-0
Library of Congress Control Number: 2012945243
Printed in 2013

Dean L. Lunt, publisher

Many Thanks to those who helped
make this book possible. Folks like Tori Britton,
Mark Wellman, Sandy Flewelling, Heidi Murphy,
Dean Lunt, Karen Hoots, Melissa Hayes, David Grima,
Katy England, Michael Fern, and Mary.

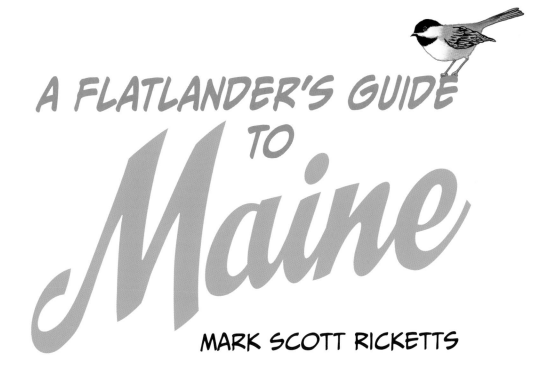

A FLATLANDER'S GUIDE TO Maine

MARK SCOTT RICKETTS

Menu

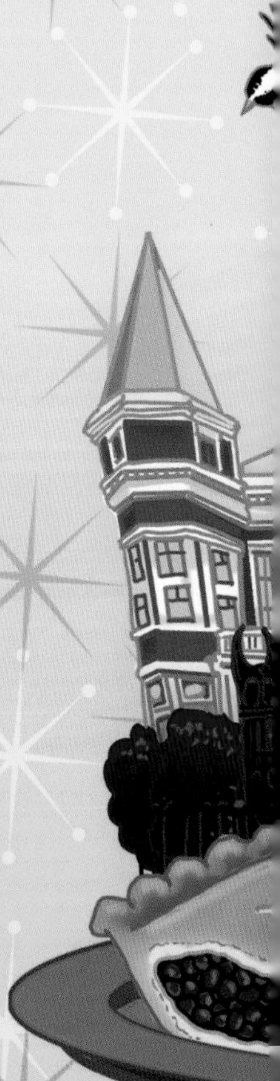

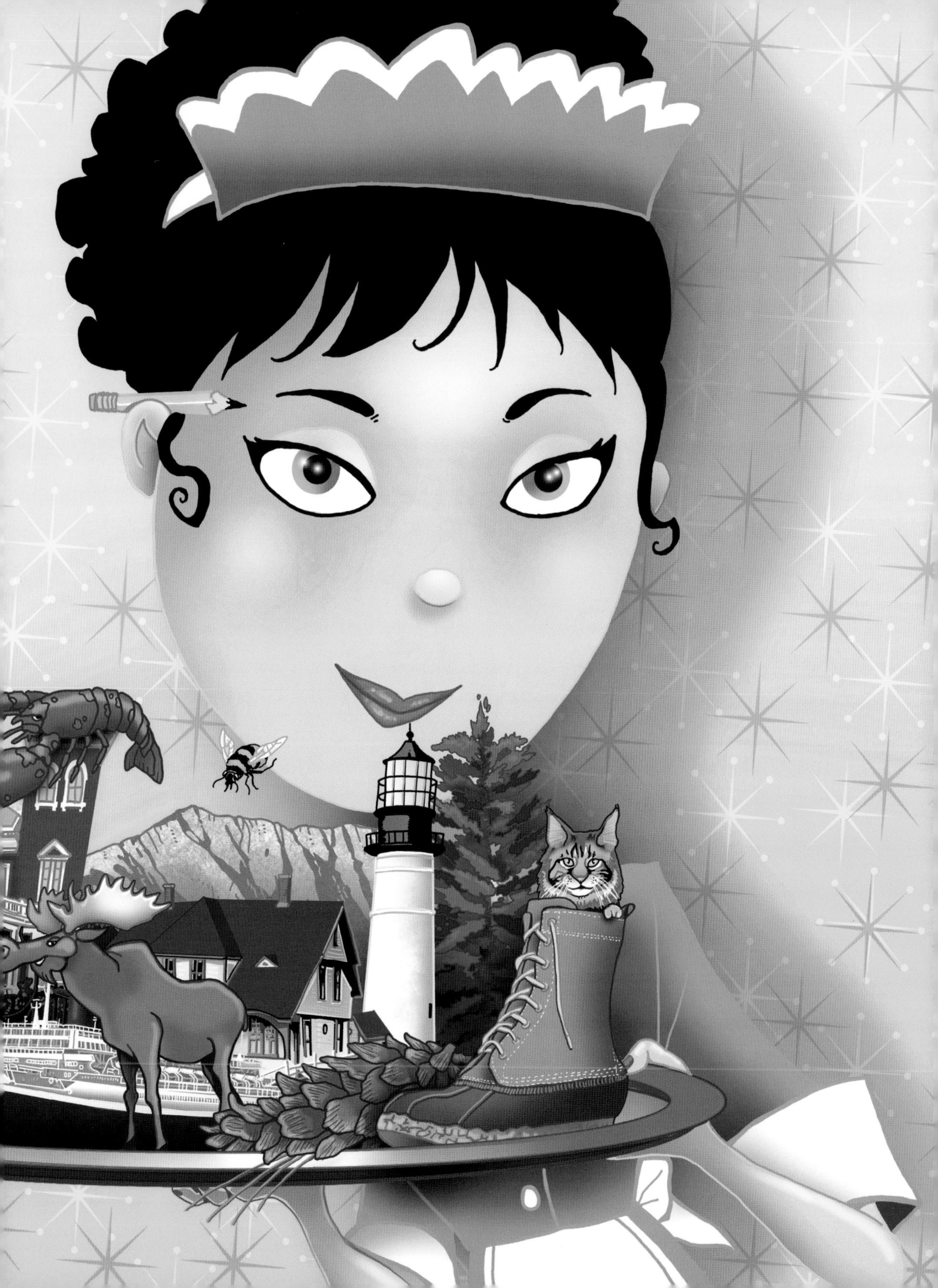

Hi, my name is Mark and I am a . . .

Flatlander!

*N*ot that long ago, my wife and I dreamed about what it would be like to move from our home in Chicago to the mythical, magical kingdom of Maine with its unspoiled beauty, tree-littered mountains, glorious waterways, and rocky coast. So, without ever actually stepping foot in the Pine Tree State, we packed up our cat and moved to historic Bangor, aka the Queen City.

The first morning in our new home I made my way downtown to Central Street. Curiosity and the smell of fresh bread drew me into the Friars' Bakehouse. While I waited for Brother Don to fetch me a cup of coffee and a blueberry muffin, a man stepped up beside me.

"You're not from here," he declared.

I smiled at the fella and proudly replied, "Just moved here."

"You don't know 'bout the winters, do you?" he asked with a grim expression.

"No. Not really. But they can't be any worse than Chicago winters," I replied.

And that's when he proceeded to tell me everything needed to "survive" the upcoming Maine winter.

First, he told me to buy a pickax and dynamite.

"The ax'll help you break the coat of ice, to get at the snow, to shovel your driveway," he said, his arm on my shoulder. "The dynamite is for clearing the snow drifts from your front porch. Last year, the drifts got up as high as twenty feet or more."

While I choked on a bit of muffin, he also cautioned me about summers. The man described some kind of bloodsucking, winged monster as big as a Chihuahua and twice as mean. Called them . . . blackflies.

"Saw one pick up a small child and fly it back to its nest," he said.

He also warned me about the moose population: "They be crazy. Never know when one might jump up out of nowhere, take a run at your car, and just RAM IT! Shredded metal. Glass. Antlers. A real mess."

Well, that fella, he just about scared me half to death. But the funny thing is, I found out later that this man who was so intent on frightening me, well, he wasn't even a native Mainer. He wasn't from Maine at all. He was from Massachusetts! So, suffice it to say, his depiction of Maine life turned out to be wildly exaggerated. Typical flatlander — totally clueless. Except that bit about the moose. Ayuh, they DO be crazy!

Recovering Flatlander

THE AUTHOR

Mark Scott Ricketts is not from Maine. He's from away. He is not a sociologist, either. He's just an out-of-stater who moved to Maine and fell in love with the place and the people. For the past few years, he's researched and explored the Pine Tree State. He now feels compelled to share his discoveries with his own kind. Sure, he gets a few things wrong every once in a while, but he means well. We forgive him, because he's just a flatlander. He really doesn't know any better.

4

Earl Hornswaggle

Earl claims to be the oldest man in Maine, clocking in, according to him, at a spry 123 years old. And that is one of his tamer assertions. Find yourself sucked into his gravity, and he will regale you with tales from his days as a lumber baron, schoolteacher, river driver, newspaperman, ferry operator, inventor, and escape artist.

Ranger Dickie Todd

Ranger Todd is a dedicated and earnest but overburdened ranger at a park in Maine. Every day, Ranger Todd contends with eccentric, anthropomorphic wildlife and obnoxious campers. He currently shares a house in Bar Harbor with a beaver named Orson.

The Maine Aptitude Test

The following is a standardized test soon to be required for admission to the great state of Maine. This test was carefully developed by a board of edj'catahs who claim that it can determine whether or not a flatlander is ready for release into the wild to mingle with the locals.

1. Folks from away who visit Maine are commonly known as:
   a. Flatlanders
   b. Tourists
   c. Summer Complaints
   d. "&#%!@!!! "
   e. All of the above

2. Folks from away who settle down in Maine are commonly known as:
   a. Transplants
   b. Carpetbaggers
   c. Plaintiffs
   d. Them people up the road with strange notions
   e. "&#%!@!!! "
   f. All of the above

3. Finish this sentence: "A true Mainer never. . .
   a. takes the snow tires off a vehicle."
   b. takes down Christmas decorations."
   c. pronounces the 'R' sound."
   d. speaks kindly of the New York Yankees."
   e. pronounces the word 'good' with one syllable (i.e., goo-ud)."
   f. All of the above

4. On any given day, a Mainer might refer to his wife as:
   a. Shade in the summer
   b. Mother
   c. Warmth come winter
   d. All of the above

5. Upwardly mobile Mainers. . .
   a. mount snowplows on their cars.
   b. refer to their dog as their navigator, advisor, and/or co-chairman.
   c. list their oil company as a dependent on their taxes.
   d. dress out a suit and tie with a plaid shirt.
   e. have their gone fishin signs professionally lettered.
   f. All of the above

6. Complete this sentence. "If my cat had kittens in the oven. . .
   a. that doesn't make them biscuits."
   b. don't ask what's for supper."
   c. you'll find me at Moody's."
   d. I'd best remember to tell Mother."
   f. All of the above

7. Finish this sentence: "You can't get there. . .
   a. so why bother."
   b. in a town car."
   c. if the ferry's out and you're not much of a swimmer."
   d. from here."
   e. 'less you pay the toll."
   f. All of the above

8. Which of these things can be found inside every true Mainer's home:
   a. Mayonnaise
   b. Pickled or frozen fiddleheads
   c. A copy of Uncle Henry's with lots of red circles
   d. Used scratch tickets
   e. All of the above

9. Complete this slogan: "Maine. . .
   a. the way life should be."
   b. is closed for repairs."
   c. is for Mainers; everybody else get out!"
   d. hopes you'll drop by, purchase, and haul away the stuff we don't want."
   e. is wicked beautiful, but wicked cold most the year."
   f. All of the above

ANSWERS: 1. e, 2. f, 3. f, 4. d, 5. f, 6. f, 7. f, 8. e, 9. f

Maine Lingo

1. Dite:
a. An insect
b. A small portion
c. A fur-lined hat

2. Spleeny:
a. Spiteful
b. Overly sensitive
c. Invertebrate

3. Ayuh:
a. Yes
b. Oxygen
c. All of the above

4. Dooryard:
a. A secret garden
b. The front yard
c. A measurement

5. Mud Season:
a. An ice cream treat
b. The period between winter and early summer
c. State elections

6. Jeezely:
a. Gristle
b. Sordid
c. Irritating

7. Pot:
a. Marijuana
b. A lobster trap
c. The convenience by your bedside

8. Jizzicked:
a. Goosed
b. Invigorated
c. Broken

9. Downcellar:
a. Hell
b. The basement
c. Your backside

10. Wicked:
a. Evil
b. Very
c. All of the above

11. Got Done:
a. Fired; laid off
b. To be schooled
c. Overcooked

12. Gawmy:
a. Clumsy
b. High humidity
c. Dumbstruck

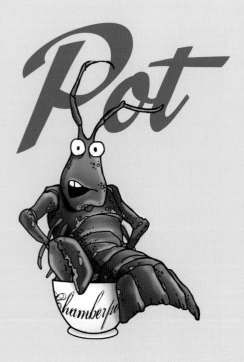

ANSWERS:
1. b. 2. b. 3. a. 4. b. 5. b. 6. c.
7. b. 8. c. 9. b. 10. c. 11. a. 12. a.

RANGER TODD'S REAL MAINE QUIZ!

Which of these images is not what it claims to be?

A STATE CAT

B STATE CONDIMENT

KRAP FAT FREE MAYO

C STATE BERRY

THAT'S WHAT HAPPENS WHEN BLUEBERRIES GROW WILD.

WOO HOO!

XXX

ANSWER: **B**

FAT FREE CONDIMENTS CAN NOT BE FOUND IN NEW ENGLAND CUISINE.

RANGER TODD'S REAL MAINE QUIZ!

Which of these images is not what it claims to be?

A STATE TREE

B STATE SCENT

C STATE ANIMAL

ANSWER: **A**

THERE ARE LOTS OF BEECH TREES IN MAINE, BUT THE EASTERN WHITE PINE IS THE STATE TREE.

Congratulations!

YOU ARE NOW PREPARED TO TRAVEL THROUGH THE PINE TREE STATE.

For further instruction continue to next page . . .

Say what?

RIVER DRIVE You probably think this refers to a scenic drive down a stretch of road with views of a river. In actuality, it's the method lumberjacks used to transport logs downriver to a sawmill. I'm told that if you can keep your balance while floating on a log, it's a pretty good way to take in the beauty of the Pine Tree State.

Traveling Maine

MAINE ROAD

a.

▼ HERE

THERE ▲

b.

c.

$

d.

e.

f.

Match the sign with its meaning

__ Tourist trap.

__ Buckle up, strap on headgear, insert mouthguard, hold on to your dash, and prepare for impact!

__ Winter around the bend.

__ Bean supper.

__ Blackfly crossing.

__ You can't get there from here.

Overturned Tractor-Trailer — 8 MI.

Yard Sale — 15 MI.

Recurring Roadwork — 20 MI.

Pothole Canyon — 23 MI.

Poor Cell Reception — 27 MI.

Slow Moving Mobile Home — 29 MI.

Gravel Pit — 32 MI.

Haunted Paper Mill — 46 MI.

Getting Lost

The state of Maine prides itself on having some of the most aggravating directional signs in the country, and for GOOD REASON. You see, making sure tourists get themselves lost and frustrated is a big part of the state's economic stimulation plan.

Travelers on their way to one of Maine's more popular spots get turned around by confusing or missing signage and invariably wind up at one of the state's humblest diners, bars, or mom 'n' pop stores looking for direction. That's how out-of-the-way shopkeepers snag their prey! Like lobsters to bait. And they don't cut 'em loose until the cash register rings.

Now, the muckety-mucks in Augusta aren't likely to 'fess up to this trick, but believe me, that's how the trap is set.

Welcome to Vacationland!

NOTE: While driving through Maine, you may experience unexplained trouble with your GPS system. The Board of Tourism reports that this interference is due to Maine's dense tree population. *Right; sure it is!*

"GEEZERS"

IN MAINE FOLKLORE, MANY STORIES ARE TOLD OF CRAFTY GEEZERS WHO LAY IN WAIT AT GAS STATIONS AND GENERAL STORES JUST TO TAUNT LOST TOURISTS. AND OVER THE YEARS, MAINE HUMORISTS HAVE ENCOURAGED THIS KIND OF BEHAVIOR. FUNNY THING IS, HARASSED TOURISTS FIND THIS PRACTICE QUAINT AND CONTINUE TO FLOCK TO THE STATE LIKE FLEAS TO A DOG. WON'T BE LONG BEFORE FOLKS UP AT THE STATE CAPITAL FORCE LOCALS TO GIVE OUT-OF-STATERS A HARD TIME...UNDER PENALTY OF LAW.

Extra Tourist-rial

*I*t was 1954 the night me 'n' my dog Salty got stuck up the tote road on our way home from the Timber! Tavern. That beat-down path was a shortcut to my trailer most the year, but even a Sherman tank would have trouble passin' that way durin' mud season—which it was. Shoulda known better, but there we were, up t' our headlights in mud. No way we were goin' nowheres, 'least anytime soon, so Salty and me found a station on the radio and settled in for the night.

Somewhere past midnight's when it come up on us—a big blast o' bright light. Then the radio went dead and the truck took to shakin'. For a moment, it felt like the Bangor & Aroostook train was chuggin' our way. Salty commenced to yelpin' while I muckled down, waitin' for whatever-the-heck-that-was to crash into us. But there wunt no crash. Just more light. Bright as heaven, I'd bet. White as snow. So danged bright you couldn't see your boots to tie the laces.

Salty growled as the cause of all this commotion rolled up to the truck. And then, there it was, big as life. Looked half-man and half-octopus. Had a mess o' long, rangy legs and this one dewy eyeball that rolled 'round its big blue noggin.

Now, I've seen some ugly critters in these parts afore, but no moose or lobster could hold a candle to this cuss. And it sure wunt local. Had to be an alien from another world.

Had a DeLorme map with it, so I guess it musta got itself lost. And it was pointin' at a certain spot on that map, too. You know, like a tourist'll do when they ask for directions. Well, sir, opportunity like this only comes along maybe once or twice in a Mainer's lifetime, so I mustered up my thickest accent, tryin' like the devil not to crack a smile, and right there and then, I tol' that alien fella, 'Sorry, chummy. You can't get they-ah from heah!"

—Earl Hornswaggle

TRAFFIC ADVISORY

Choose the right word to complete the sentence.

1. Those not acquainted with the quaint motoring customs of _____ are thrown by a disregard for turn signals.

a. student drivers **b. ATV drivers** **c. Mainers**

2. World-weary _____ may decide to take a simultaneous cigarette break, holding up traffic.

a. road workers **b. beavers** **c. toll collectors**

3. An errant bull moose during _____ season considers your vehicle a threat to his masculinity and forces you into a duel.

a. mud **b. hunting** **c. rutting**

4. The psychedelic effect of _____ causes mass hallucination and a multi-vehicle pileup.

a. skunk spray **b. undulating road** **c. fall foliage**

The answer to each question is C.

Say what?

THE GRANGE The Grange movement was a farmers' association created in 1867. In the beginning, many Maine farming towns erected buildings known as Grange Halls to provide a place for the Order of the Patrons of Husbandry to perform strange rituals with small ornamental farm tools. It fell out of favor, as Maine farmers were too busy to learn secret passwords and handshakes. Today, many of these old structures are beyond repair, but those still standing hold bean suppers, contra dances, auctions, and flea markets.

Maine History

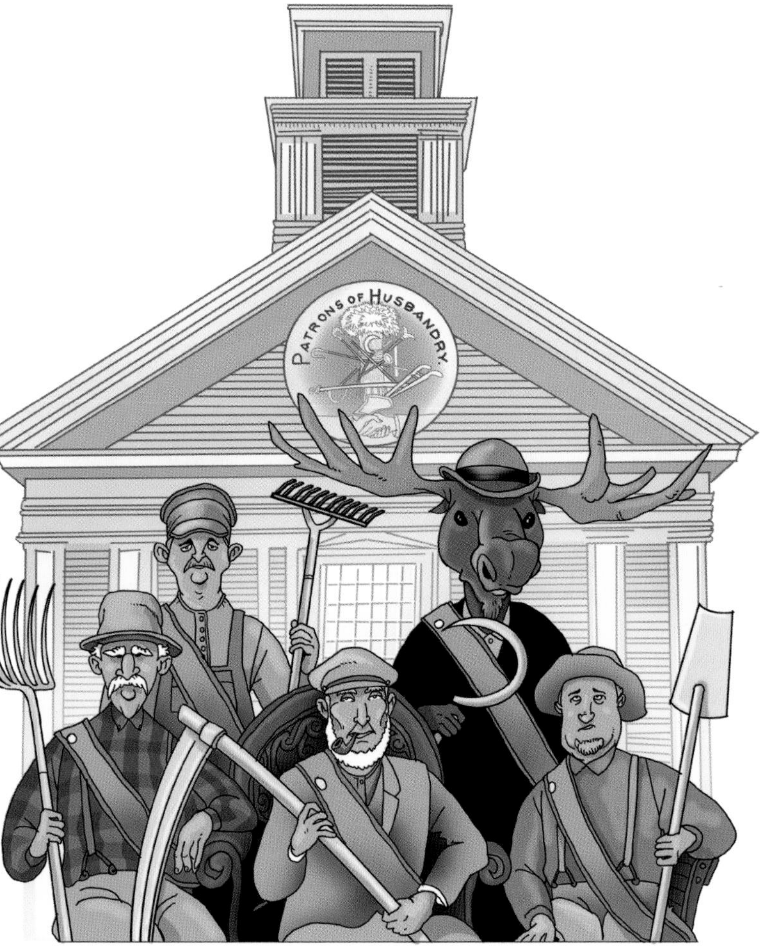
PATRONS OF HUSBANDRY

MAINE HISTORY TIMELINE

{ *First FLATLANDER to land on Maine soil.* }

15,000 years ago. Glacial landforms create Maine coast. Paleo-Indian tribe sees no future in the real estate market and sticks to hunting and gathering.

1000 AD. After a night of grog and bad clams, hallucinating Vikings fight off phantom ice demons and sea monsters. With no one to man the long ship, they eventually crash into the Maine coast. Delusional Vikings leave a bad impression on the natives and set the inhospitable tone for future relations with tourists.

1497. European explorers claim discovery of the Maine coast where they encounter hostile, name-calling tribes, angry moose, and hideously ugly crustaceans. The weather wasn't exactly accommodating either.

1524. Italian explorer and trinket trader Giovanni da Verrazzano is mooned by rude natives at a landfall he names Bare Bottom. Sanctimonious mapmakers rename the landfall Bald Head.

There was a time when the lobster wasn't considered food, much less a delicacy. It was used for fertilizer! However, local fishermen got the idea to sell lobster to tourists for top dollar. They called it luxury food, the region's finest cuisine. And the tourists gobbled it up.

FLATLANDERS'LL EAT ANYTHING IF YOU SERVE IT WITH CORN.

1604. For a laugh, explorers spread rumors of a city made of gold named Norumbega located on the Maine coast. Greedy but gullible sailors launched expeditions.

1774. During the Revolutionary War, a mob burns shipment of tea in York, Maine. Boston warns them to be prepared for caffeine withdrawal.

1775. British soldiers burn Falmouth to the ground for two points. The Maine team rallies and captures a British cutter before halftime.

1781. The British army tearfully take their football and go home.

1820. Massachusetts can't take Maine anywhere without being embarrassed. To enhance their street cred, Massachusetts disses Maine in public and cuts them loose. Maine, now a free state, bids a traditional farewell to Massachusetts by dropping trouser and mooning them.

1834. The lumber boom begins with a tavern fight.

1838. Canada mows the lawn over its boundary in an attempt to move the property line. Maine plays its music too loud at all hours during the work week and backs up its wagons in Canada's driveway. Canada eventually gives up and stays on its own side.

1851. The Maine Law is passed, making Maine the first state in the union to ban the manufacture and sale of alcohol. This prompts a little dustup called the Portland Rum Riot. Days later, rioters revealed that street brawling is not as much fun when you're sober.

Throughout Maine's history, public drunkenness and brawling has been a popular pastime. Back in the 1800s, If you didn't wake up in the jailhouse with a missing tooth on Sunday morning, you just weren't living up to your potential.

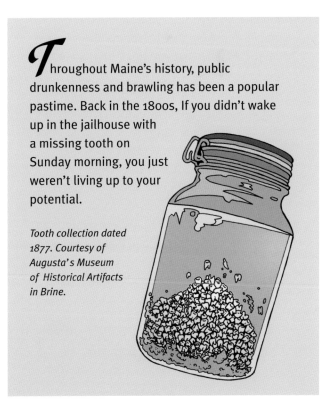

Tooth collection dated 1877. Courtesy of Augusta's Museum of Historical Artifacts in Brine.

I'm 'shamed to say it, but I do believe my Uncle Ellis was the cause of that tragic fire in 1911. Yes sir, it was suppah time, and according to my father, Uncle Ellis near finished off a whole pot o' beans up t' Widow Lumper's bed-and-breakfast.

Afterwards, the two of 'em went to check on their mule out the hay shed on Broad Street. Then it come up on Uncle Ellis, a familiar rumblin' t' his backside. Well sir, the way I heard it, wunt long 'fore he cut the cheese. That wunt the end of it, neither. Next time he got the urge, Uncle Ellis fired up a match, bent over, and positioned the flame up t' his hindquarter. According to my father, once Uncle Ellis let the next one loose, flame sprayed out at least three feet. Hay took spark. Pretty soon the whole town lit up like a Christmas tree. When the smoke cleared, and Bangor officials decided the fire started in that ol' hay shed, blame fell on the donkey. After some thought and a thorough examination, it was concluded that the mule kicked over an oil lamp. When questioned, both my father and my uncle claimed it was indeed an ass what caused that terrible tragedy.

—Earl Hornswaggle

1856. The Maine Law is repealed. Celebrating Mainers have to be peeled off the sidewalk next morning.

1863. Joshua Chamberlain defends Little Round Top against Confederate troops at the Battle of Gettysburg during the Civil War. On that very day, he also defends his silly mustache when teased by his superiors.

1876. The soft drink Moxie is created in Union, Maine. Calvin Coolidge liked it. Need we say more?

1912. European-styled-footwear is much too delicate for Maine's rocky terrain, much less the soggy parts. Enter L.L. Bean.

1915. Deer Isle celebrates first Lupine Festival. Werewolves mistakenly fill surrounding hotels and B&Bs, making it impossible for flower enthusiasts to find a vacancy.

1917. L.L. Bean sets up Freeport store. Catalogs are mailed all over the country.

1918. The Bean boot is wildly successful. Catalog production increases.

1929. Lafayette National Park changes its name to Acadia. Alternative name, Bob's Oasis, comes in a close second.

1947. Bar Harbor residents incinerate the heaps of L.L. Bean catalogs they'd been receiving in the mail since 1912. A devastating forest fire destroys a good deal of Mount Desert Island.

1949. A roadside geezer confuses traveling flatlanders with perplexing directions. A state pastime is established.

1952. The first lobster-trap coffee table is sold to a vacationing couple from Detroit. When word of this transaction spreads, gift shops pop up all over the state.

1959. Wolf population decides Maine is not worth the trouble and moves on.

1973. Miss Deb Barnacle crowned Caribou's first (and last) Duct Tape Queen.

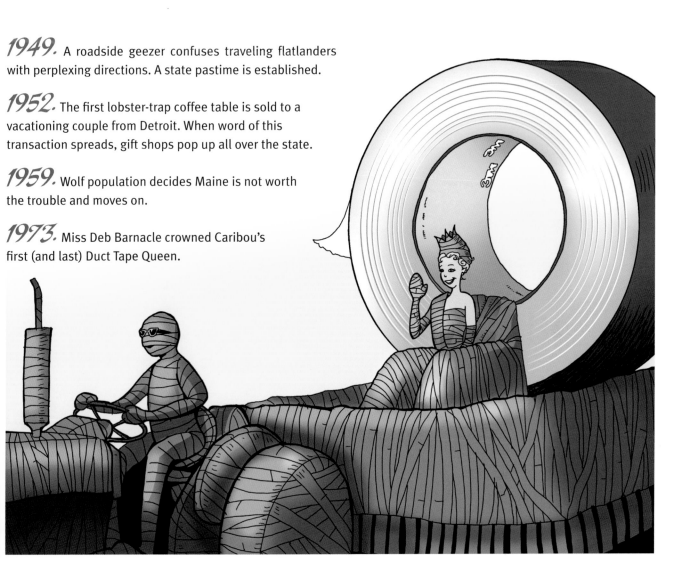

1986. A restaurant specializing in Manhattan clam chowder opens for lunch in Augusta. Closes an hour later.

1990. The Running of the Bulls in Palmyra takes place. Similar to the event in Pamplona, except, in this case, the bulls were actually three nearsighted moose.

1998. An ice storm transforms Maine into a glacier, making it appear as it once did 15,000 years ago.

2000. Maine introduces a law banning derogatory town names. LazyGut Island refuses to comply.

2010. Law passes granting the right to possess firearms in Acadia National Park.

Say what?

AYUH This is **THE** most important word in a Mainer's vocabulary. It means "YES," but when spoken by one who understands the nuances in its presentation, its meaning can either be comforting or condesending. *WARNING: This word is unpronounceable to those not born and raised in New England. Flatlanders should NOT, under any circumstance, attempt to utter this word. To a Mainer, improper pronunciation of this word is eqivalent to fingernails scraping a chalkboard.*

Maine Culture

AY
UH

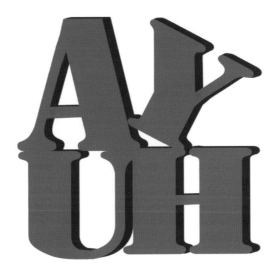

LODGING

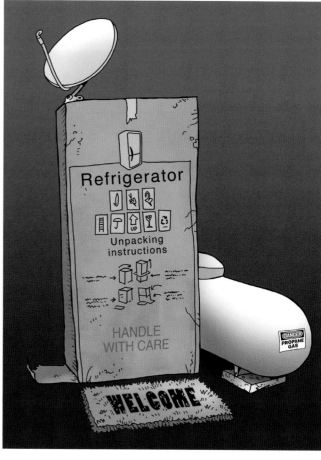

*Y*ou'll find some really beautiful, classic homes in Maine. But traditional accommodations aren't for everyone. Some Mainers prefer what you might call alternative living spaces.

Heckuva View

Back in the 1800s, timbah tycoons **Samuel Veazie** and **Timothy Crosby** was the kings of Bangor. Thing is, you can't have two kings rulin' one kingdom. Won't do. That's why they were always in a tussle. Ayuh, those fellas fought like jealous twins reachin' for the last piece of chicken at suppah. One time, Crosby got his undies in a twist 'cause Veazie's house blocked his view of the Penobscot River, so he just up and sued him. When that didn't pan out, Crosby added two more floors to his house outta spite. Not to be topped, Veazie built his place up even higher. AND ON IT WENT—till them feudahs added about thirty stories between 'em. But just like the tower of Babel, those two gangly structures crashed to the ground. All it took was a good stiff wind. When the dust settled, Crosby rebuilt. But Veazie refused to live anywhere near his rival, so he carved off a piece of Bangor, built a *brand new* town, named it after himself, and drafted a law* forbiddin' entry to anyone named Crosby, lest they be shot on sight.

* Someone might want to check to see if that law is still on the books.

—*Earl Hornswaggle*

MAINE'S ENTREPRENEURIAL SPIRIT

*M*ainers are clever. And they like to tinker too. Of course, not all things made in Maine are quite as useful as the toothpick, the lobster-trap coffee table, or the doughnut-hole machine. In fact, some of the thingamajigs, doohickeys, and gizmos created in the Pine Tree State are just downright irresponsible.

OH SURE, OL' CHESTER GREENWOOD DID A FINE THING WHEN HE COME UP WITH THE EAR MUFFLER. BUT THAT WUNT THE *ONLY* THING HE INVENTED.

United States Patent Office

Bustle Muffler
No. 188.297

Fig. 1

Claw Muffler
No. 188.298

Fig. 1

Nose Muffler
No. 188.296

Fig. 1

Bran Muffin
with Dual Exhaust Mufflers
No. 188.299

Fig. 1

Potholes in Maine are as deep as a dinosaur footprint and mean as a rutting bull moose. Now, some just chew on your tires. But they've been known to swallow whole town cars and burp up scrap metal. So before one of those craters snaps at the axle on your pickup this year, spring into action with . . .

The mud in Maine is a lot like quicksand, except it's chock-full of clay. And when the ground thaws after winter, that sticky muck will strip the Christmas shoes right off your feet. So if you're sick of getting a sinking feeling every mud season and you're fed up with tippytoeing across wood gangplanks to get from your dooryard to your truck, I've got just the thing . . .

The
Mudslappah
3000

Rangers tell tourists to take only pictures, but you can't walk the Maine woods without coming home with something else—itchy welts from minges, blackflies, and mosquitoes. Well, you can quit your scratching and moaning, because it's time to "bite back" with . . .

MAINE ART

Mona Lobstah

Christina's Standpipe

Warhol's Bean Boot

Tip NEVER MAKE FUN OF A CHAIN-SAW SCULPTURE WITHIN EARSHOT OF THE ARTIST.

During the 125th anniversary of Bangor's incorporation as a city, a statue of Paul Bunyan was unveiled on lower Main Street. However, it was not the only sculpture considered to represent Bangor. Here are some designs that were rejected.

MAINE FASHION

Maine haute couture often consists of something plaid, Bean boots, a barn coat, and a hat with fuzzy ear flaps. Axes make great accessories, but are not essential when creating an ensemble.

CAUTION: Mainers have been known to wear shorty shorts and flip-flops in temperatures slightly above 40 degrees. This is not recommended for folks not acclimated to cold climates.

IF YOU WEAR BUNNY SLIPPERS DURING RABBIT MATING SEASON, YOU'RE JUST ASKING FOR TROUBLE.

WELL, *HEL-LO, LADIES!*

HOOVES AND HEELS ARE A SHAKY COMBINATION.

ANTLERS ARE NOT COAT RACKS. NOR DO I RECOMMEND YOU HANG JEWELRY, CHRISTMAS LIGHTS, OR NOVELTY AIR FRESHENERS ON THEM.

AWW, GEE, NOT *AGAIN!*

CARNIVORES SHOULD NEVER EVER WEAR WHITE.

WEARING A MINK FUR COAT AND BLING DOES NOT MAKE YOU GANGSTA.

FISHNET STOCKINGS ARE NOT FOR FISH.

TANNED HIDE AND LEATHER IS A BIG FASHION DON'T. AFTER ALL, YOU MIGHT BE RELATED TO THE ORIGINAL OWNER.

PRETTY NICE FOR A HAND-ME-DOWN, DON'T YA THINK?

NEVER WEAR APPAREL WITH THE TARGET LOGO ON IT. ESPECIALLY DURING HUNTING SEASON.

DRESS THE MAINER!

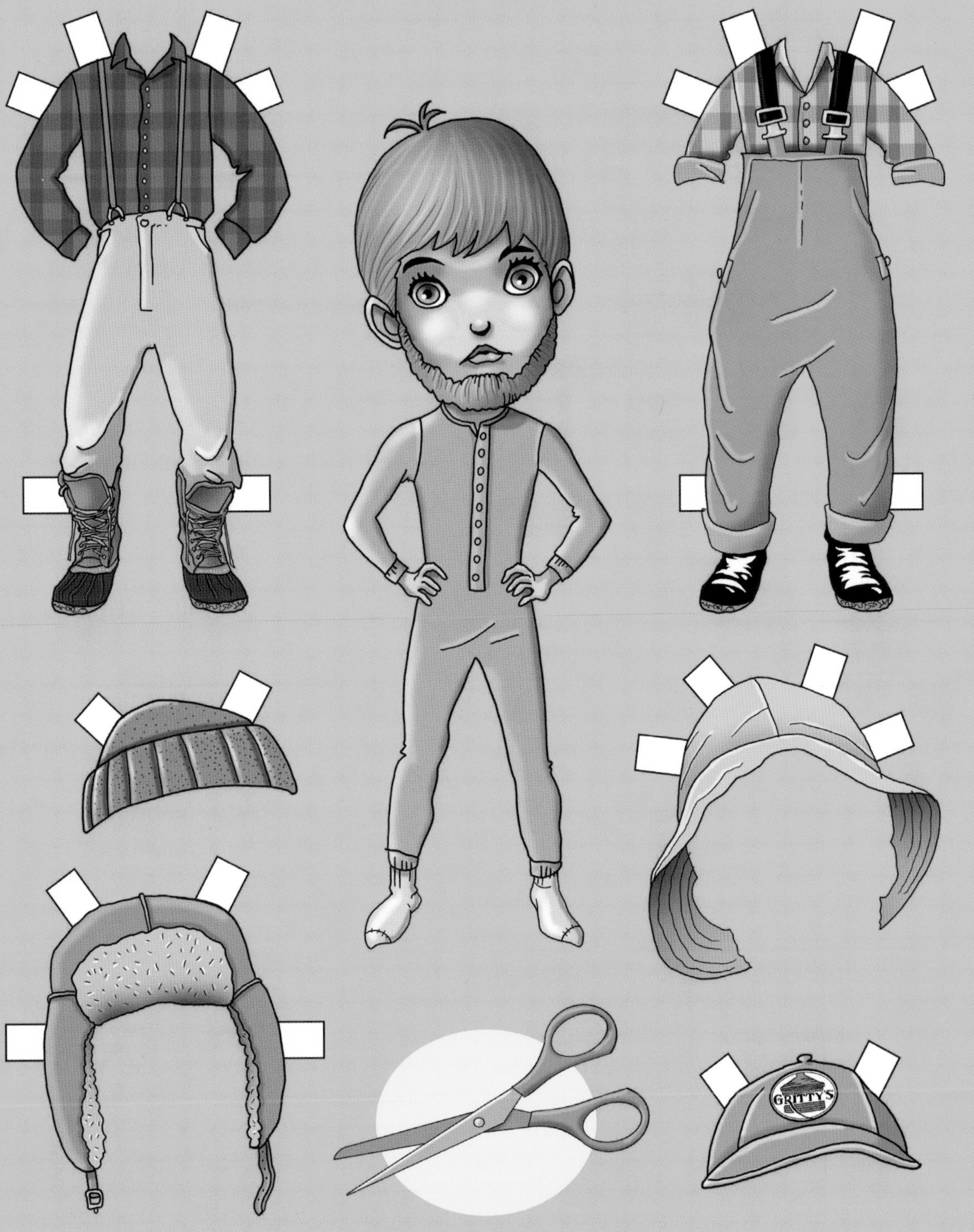
GRITTY'S

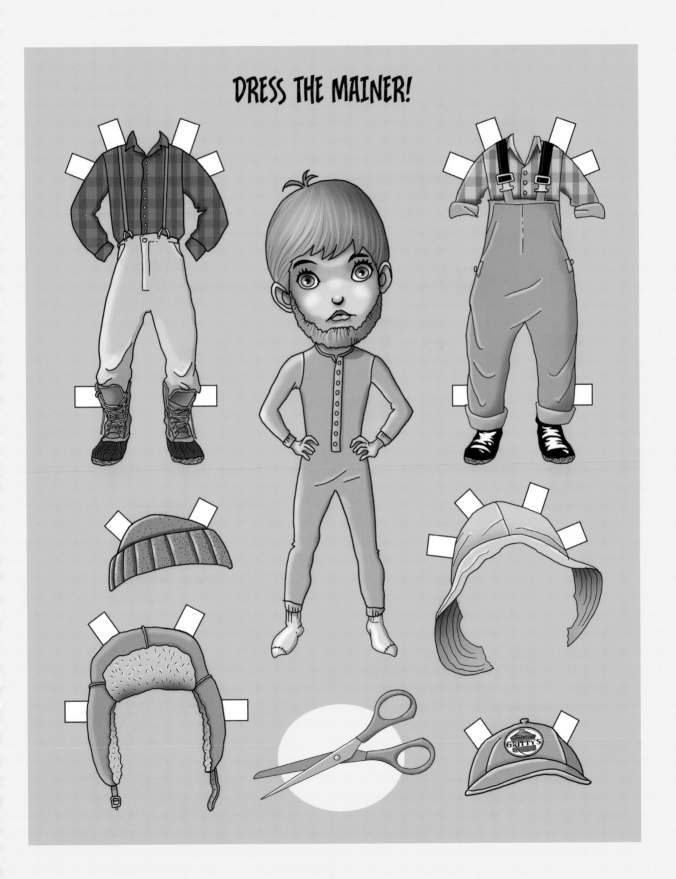

EXTRA CREDIT

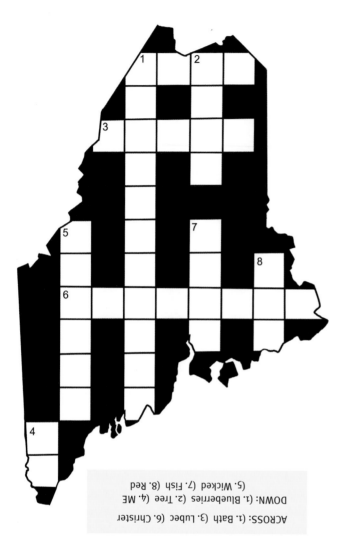

ACROSS: (1. Bath (3. Lubec (6. Christer
DOWN: (1. Blueberries (2. Tree (4. ME
(5. Wicked (7. Fish (8. Red)

ACROSS

1 The place known as the city of ships. Also, what you'll need after a day pulling your truck out of the muck come mud season.

3 The folks in this town were once conned into believing gold could be extracted from seawater. And no, we're not talking about lobsters.

6 That big idea you had, the storm you weathered, and the grand to-do you attended might be referred to as one of these.

DOWN

1 What Sal picked.

2 Can't go nowheres in Maine without runnin' into one of these.

4 The abbreviation for the state of Maine. Also, someone you admire.

5 If it's some ol' good, it's _ _ _ _ _ _ good!

7 Catch it. Pickle it. Batter it. Fry it. Bake it. But if you like it raw with wasabi, you've come to the wrong state. Also, that's the odor you can't seem to get out of your clothes since visiting Eastport.

8 The way folks in Maine love their hot dogs. It's also the color a lobster turns when you throw it in a hot tub. Also, it's the color of the angry fellah in that hot tub when you pitched the lobster in there.

MAINERS ARE WELL KNOWN FOR THEIR STOICISM AND LACK OF PRETENSION.

THEY DON'T TOLERATE POMPOUS BEHAVIOR EITHER. ESPECIALLY FROM ONE OF THEIR OWN.

YUH NOT FOOLIN' ANYONE, CHUMMY.

Snapshots from Maine.

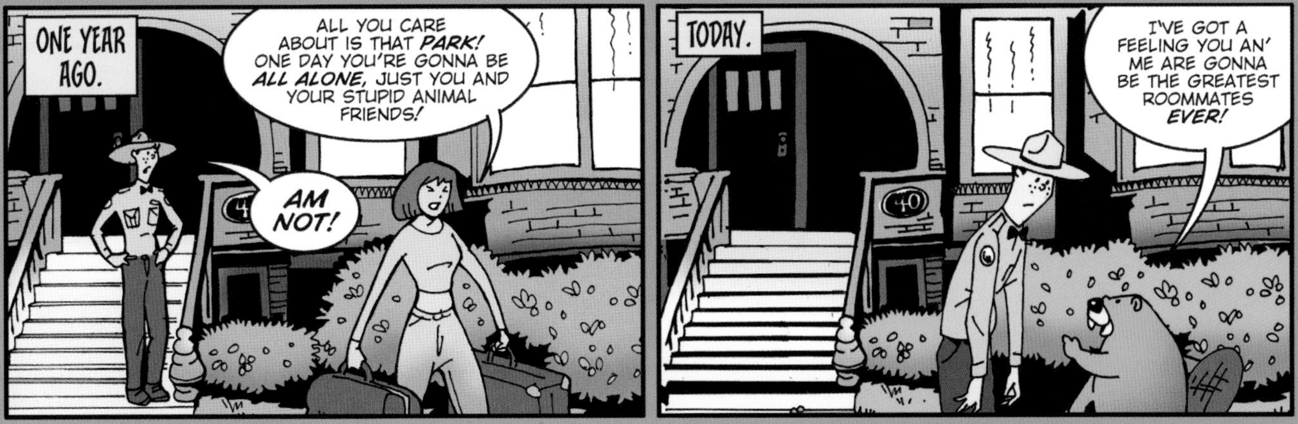
ONE YEAR AGO.
ALL YOU CARE ABOUT IS THAT PARK! ONE DAY YOU'RE GONNA BE ALL ALONE, JUST YOU AND YOUR STUPID ANIMAL FRIENDS!
AM NOT!
TODAY.
I'VE GOT A FEELING YOU AN' ME ARE GONNA BE THE GREATEST ROOMMATES EVER!

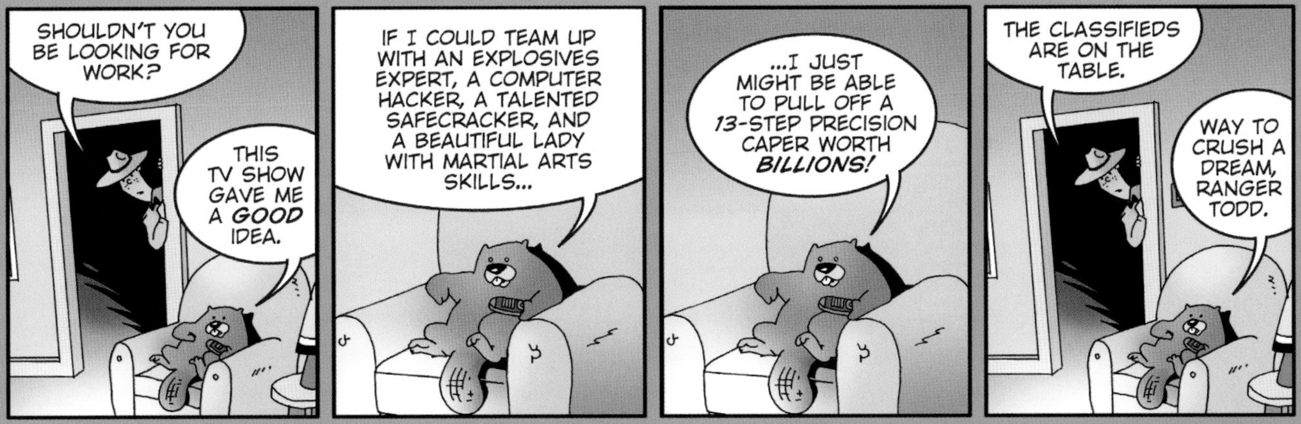
SHOULDN'T YOU BE LOOKING FOR WORK?
THIS TV SHOW GAVE ME A GOOD IDEA.
IF I COULD TEAM UP WITH AN EXPLOSIVES EXPERT, A COMPUTER HACKER, A TALENTED SAFECRACKER, AND A BEAUTIFUL LADY WITH MARTIAL ARTS SKILLS...
...I JUST MIGHT BE ABLE TO PULL OFF A 13-STEP PRECISION CAPER WORTH BILLIONS!
THE CLASSIFIEDS ARE ON THE TABLE.
WAY TO CRUSH A DREAM, RANGER TODD.

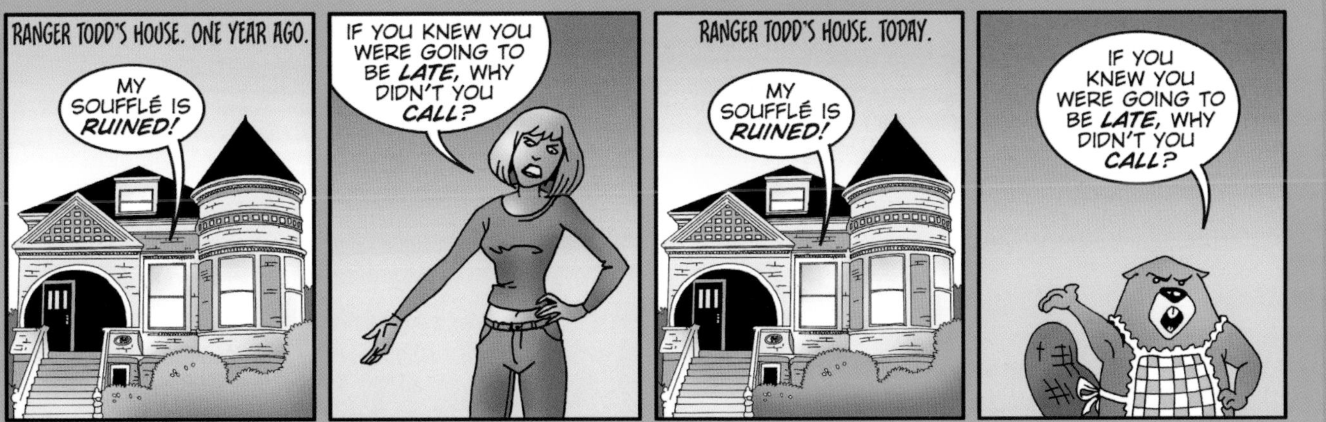
RANGER TODD'S HOUSE. ONE YEAR AGO.
MY SOUFFLÉ IS RUINED!
IF YOU KNEW YOU WERE GOING TO BE LATE, WHY DIDN'T YOU CALL?
RANGER TODD'S HOUSE. TODAY.
MY SOUFFLÉ IS RUINED!
IF YOU KNEW YOU WERE GOING TO BE LATE, WHY DIDN'T YOU CALL?

Say what?

HAKE According to Mainers, this is a particularly stupid fish. Not sure why they consider this fish to be any more stupid than, say, a splake, but they do. In fact, Mainers think so little of this fish's intelligence they've adopted the phrase "numb-er than a hake" to describe anyone who they consider to be downright dumb.

Maine Fauna

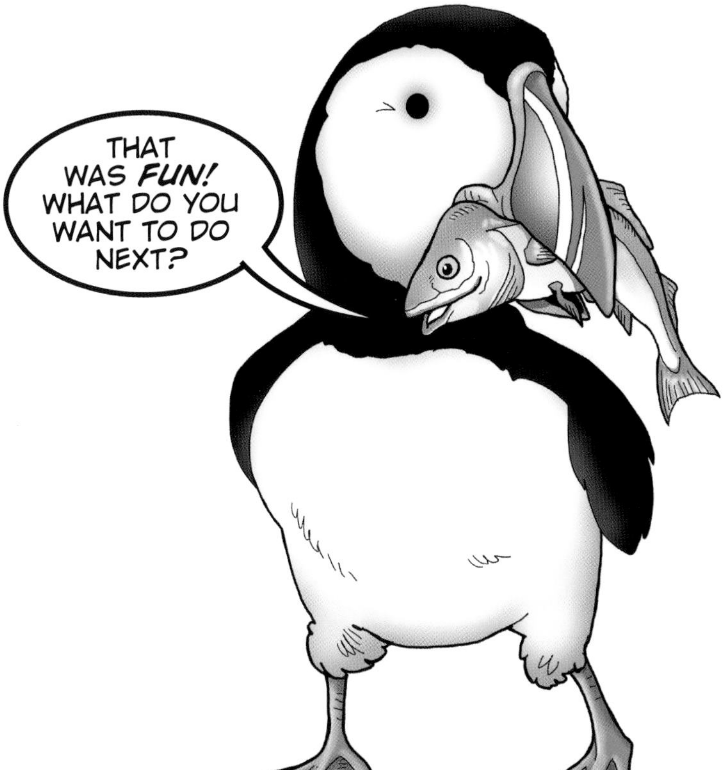
THAT WAS *FUN!* WHAT DO YOU WANT TO DO NEXT?

MOOSE

*W*hen encountering a moose in the Maine woods, suppress the urge to laugh at their gangly appearance. Sure, their spindly legs, humped back, unkempt goatee, droopy lip, long nose, and small tail are comical, but you should allow them *some* dignity. Especially if they are irritable, hormonally charged bulls equipped with 40-pound, multi-tined antlers.

If a moose attempts to engage you in conversation, stick to subjects pertaining to salt licks and the blackfly problem. If a moose is inclined to talk about his mother abandonment issues, change the subject immediately. I suggest you compliment them on their swimming abilities. Or congratulate them on their being named the official state animal of Maine. Moose love flattery, even if it's insincere.

BEAR

*W*hen encountering a bear in the Maine woods, wave your arms and speak in a normal tone of voice. Bears are usually not a threat, but they do deserve your respect.

Avoid commenting on the physical appearance of their mother. Avoid topics of a political or spiritual nature.

REALLY, MR. BEAR. I HAVE NO OPINION ON THE SUBJECT.

If a curious bear gets too close, raise your voice and make loud noises. But never ever squeal like a hyperactive kid revved up on a sugar high.

PERSONAL SPACE! PERSONAL SPACE!

EEEEE!!

LIKE I SAID BEFORE, CAMPERS AND SIGHTSEERS ARE RETURNING TO THE PARK AND WE SHOULD BE SENSITIVE TO THEIR NEEDS.

I HAVE NO IDEA WHY THAT WOMAN SCREAMED.

WHILE MANY PARK VISITORS MAY FEEL COMPELLED TO COMMUNE WITH NATURE, THEY ARE, IN FACT, WELL, LET'S JUST SAY IT... THEY'RE SLIGHTLY *BEAR*-PHOBIC.

I JUST ASKED IF SHE WAS GONNA FINISH HER SANDWICH.

I DO APPRECIATE YOUR EFFORT, BUT WHEN I TOLD YOU TO KEEP A LOW PROFILE, THIS WAS NOT EXACTLY WHAT I MEANT.

HEY, EVERYBODY LOVES HOCKEY. WHAT IF I WORE A HOCKEY MASK?

FISH

*M*ost folks don't remembah what it was like when the salmon were bountiful. It was like a gosh-darn epidemic. They were whoppin' big too. Way back in the nineteeth century, a twenty-pound salmon was thought too puny to mess with. A ninety-poundah, that was a fair catch. Some even grew big as a child raised on fried dough and whoopie pies. Those days, salmon wunt just big, they were ornery — mean as schoolyard bullies. Sometimes they'd gang up, turn over your boat, and for no good reason, slap you silly with their tails. Other times, they'd poke their heads up from the water and spit right in your eye.

—*Earl Hornswaggle*

MANY DAMS IN MAINE HAVE DEVELOPED "FISH LADDERS" AND SPECIAL ELEVATORS TO PROVIDE ATLANTIC SALMON EASY PASSAGE UPSTREAM TO THEIR SPAWNING GROUND.

DADDY'S COMIN' HOME, BABY!

PANT! PANT!

EXAMPLE ONE

COULD SOMEONE PRESS FOUR, PLEASE?

I'M LATE FOR A *BOOTY CALL!*

EXAMPLE TWO

WHAT ARE *YOU* LOOKIN' AT?

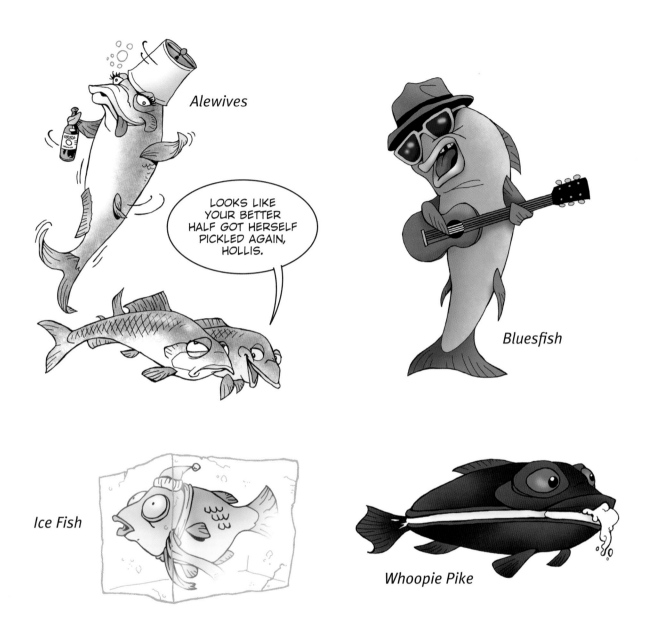

Alewives

LOOKS LIKE YOUR BETTER HALF GOT HERSELF PICKLED AGAIN, HOLLIS.

Bluesfish

Ice Fish

Whoopie Pike

NATURE IS JUST AS CURIOUS ABOUT US AS WE ARE ABOUT NATURE.

WHALE WATCHING

HEY RANDY, YOU *GOTTA* SEE THIS GUY! HE'S WEARIN' BERMUDA SHORTS WITH BLACK KNEE SOCKS AND SANDALS.

EXAMPLE 1

EXAMPLE 2

AIIEEEE!

BUGS

A Rogues' Gallery of Maine's Most Notorious Bugs

Saco Slugs

Bangor Bedbugs

C'MON, HONEY. I WON'T BITE.

Harpswell Head Lice

HAIR PEACE

Patten Potato Bugs

Blackflies

DID I TELL YA THAT BLACKFLIES ARE ATTRACTED TO COLOGNE?

BLOOD DRIVE

GIVE

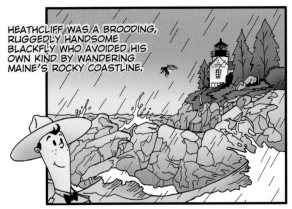

HEATHCLIFF WAS A BROODING, RUGGEDLY HANDSOME BLACKFLY WHO AVOIDED HIS OWN KIND BY WANDERING MAINE'S ROCKY COASTLINE.

THEN, SHE ENTERED HIS LIFE.

HEY THERE, SAILOR.

IT WAS LOVE AT FIRST SIGHT!

AFTER BEARING HEATHCLIFF'S 600 CHILDREN, SHE DUMPED HIM. HE'D HOPED THEY'D GROW OLD TOGETHER—AND SINCE BLACKFLIES ONLY HAVE A 3-WEEK LIFESPAN, IT'S NOT LIKE HE WAS ASKING FOR MUCH—BUT IT WAS NOT TO BE.

SHE'S A HEARTLESS BLOODSUCKER. BUT I *STILL* LOVE HER.

HEATHCLIFF THE BLACKFLY, HEARTSICK FROM HAVING LOST THE LOVE OF HIS LIFE, THREW HIMSELF ONTO THE WINDSHIELD OF A VEHICLE AND DROVE OFF INTO THE NIGHT.

AFTER A HARROWING DRIVE, HEATHCLIFF EVENTUALLY FOUND HIMSELF AMONG A SWARM OF LOVE-SCARRED DUMPSTER BARFLIES BEHIND BANGOR'S *HOLLYWOOD SLOTS* CASINO.

WAH! SHE WAS MY EVERYTHING!

UNTIL ONE DAY, A CHARISMATIC HORSEFLY TOOK OUR WRETCHED HERO UNDER HIS WING AND SHOWED HIM THE LIGHT—

WHERE?

OVER *THERE,* DUMMY.

ZZTT!

-THE BUG LIGHT!

CATS

County Cats

Coastal Cats

City Cats

DOGS

Sea Dogs

Chow Hounds

Lumber Mutts

IT'S A CANT DOG.* GET IT?

* Lumberjacks use them to roll logs.

BIRDS

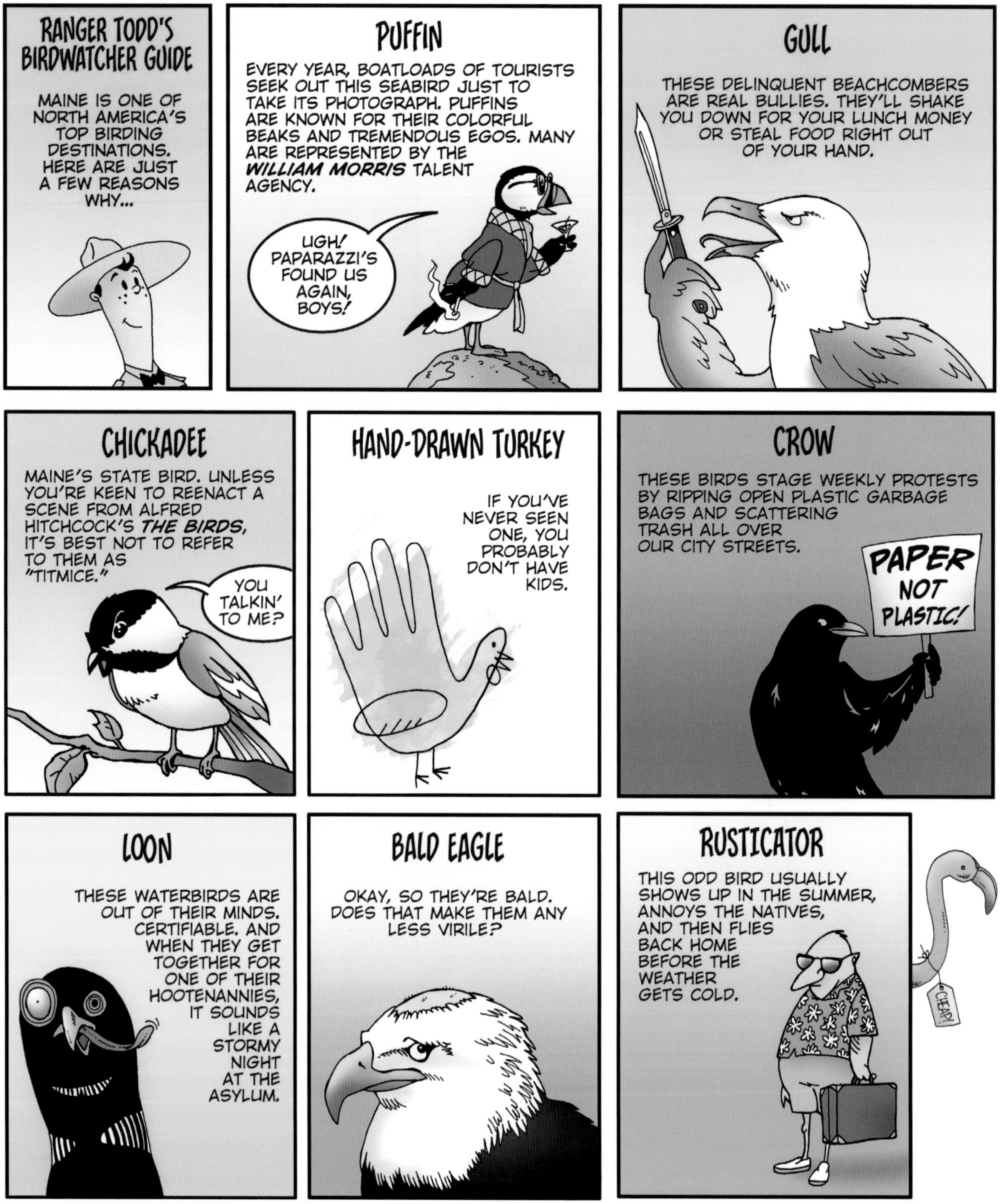
RANGER TODD'S BIRDWATCHER GUIDE
MAINE IS ONE OF NORTH AMERICA'S TOP BIRDING DESTINATIONS. HERE ARE JUST A FEW REASONS WHY...
PUFFIN
EVERY YEAR, BOATLOADS OF TOURISTS SEEK OUT THIS SEABIRD JUST TO TAKE ITS PHOTOGRAPH. PUFFINS ARE KNOWN FOR THEIR COLORFUL BEAKS AND TREMENDOUS EGOS. MANY ARE REPRESENTED BY THE *WILLIAM MORRIS* TALENT AGENCY.
UGH! PAPARAZZI'S FOUND US AGAIN, BOYS!
GULL
THESE DELINQUENT BEACHCOMBERS ARE REAL BULLIES. THEY'LL SHAKE YOU DOWN FOR YOUR LUNCH MONEY OR STEAL FOOD RIGHT OUT OF YOUR HAND.
CHICKADEE
MAINE'S STATE BIRD. UNLESS YOU'RE KEEN TO REENACT A SCENE FROM ALFRED HITCHCOCK'S *THE BIRDS*, IT'S BEST NOT TO REFER TO THEM AS "TITMICE."
YOU TALKIN' TO ME?
HAND-DRAWN TURKEY
IF YOU'VE NEVER SEEN ONE, YOU PROBABLY DON'T HAVE KIDS.
CROW
THESE BIRDS STAGE WEEKLY PROTESTS BY RIPPING OPEN PLASTIC GARBAGE BAGS AND SCATTERING TRASH ALL OVER OUR CITY STREETS.
PAPER NOT PLASTIC!
LOON
THESE WATERBIRDS ARE OUT OF THEIR MINDS. CERTIFIABLE. AND WHEN THEY GET TOGETHER FOR ONE OF THEIR HOOTENANNIES, IT SOUNDS LIKE A STORMY NIGHT AT THE ASYLUM.
BALD EAGLE
OKAY, SO THEY'RE BALD. DOES THAT MAKE THEM ANY LESS VIRILE?
RUSTICATOR
THIS ODD BIRD USUALLY SHOWS UP IN THE SUMMER, ANNOYS THE NATIVES, AND THEN FLIES BACK HOME BEFORE THE WEATHER GETS COLD.
CHEAP!

Snapshots from Maine.

HEY, RANGER TODD! MIND IF I CHECK OUT YOUR LIBRARY FOR SOMETHING TO READ?

WHAT'S THIS? *THE MATING RITUAL OF THE BLACK BEAR.*

KINKY.

SHOULDN'T YOU BE... HIBERNATING?

OOH, LISTEN TO THIS...

"THE FEMALE BEAR IS CALLED A *SOW*."

HA! LIKE A *PIG*! THAT'S FUNNY.

READ FURTHER. YOU'LL FIND A MALE BEAR'S CALLED A *BOAR*.

GEE, I ALWAYS THOUGHT OF MYSELF AS BEING *KINDA* CHARMING.

"ONCE FEMALES COME INTO SEASON...

....THEY LEAVE *SCENT* TRAILS FOR MALE BEARS TO HONE IN ON."

THE SMELL OF FRESH-BAKED *COOKIES*. THAT GETS ME *EVERY* TIME.

Say what?

PUCKERBRUSH Unidentifiable, thick, tangled underbrush growing wild along the side of Maine roads. Nobody knows where it comes from. Nobody knows what it is. Everyone just leaves it alone in fear that they may be snatched up by its prickly limbs and pulled into its terrible mess of brambles.

Maine Flora

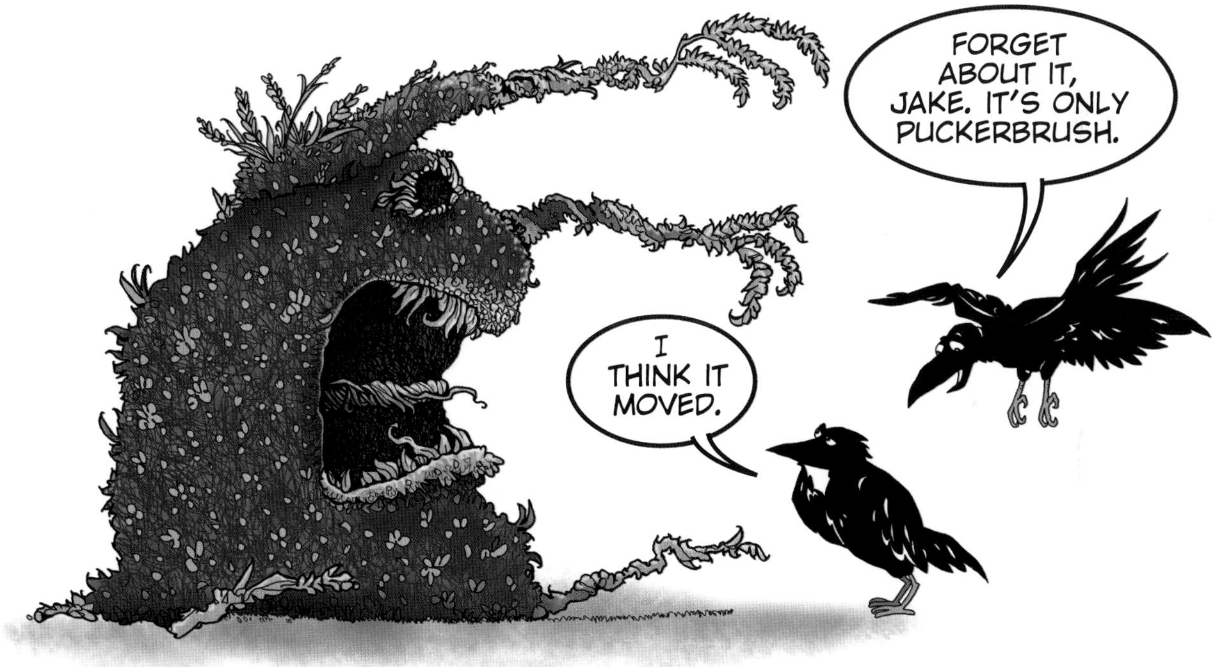
FORGET ABOUT IT, JAKE. IT'S ONLY PUCKERBRUSH.
I THINK IT MOVED.

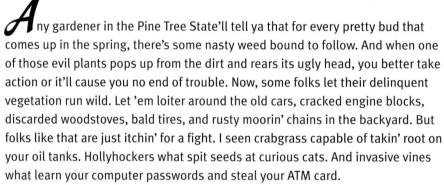

Earl Hornswaggle's GARDENING JOURNAL

*A*ny gardener in the Pine Tree State'll tell ya that for every pretty bud that comes up in the spring, there's some nasty weed bound to follow. And when one of those evil plants pops up from the dirt and rears its ugly head, you better take action or it'll cause you no end of trouble. Now, some folks let their delinquent vegetation run wild. Let 'em loiter around the old cars, cracked engine blocks, discarded woodstoves, bald tires, and rusty moorin' chains in the backyard. But folks like that are just itchin' for a fight. I seen crabgrass capable of takin' root on your oil tanks. Hollyhockers what spit seeds at curious cats. And invasive vines what learn your computer passwords and steal your ATM card.

Smart homeowners need to be on the lookout for these bad-news blooms and nip 'em in the bud. Shoot 'em fulla buckshot. Stab 'em repeatedly with a butcher knife. Wrestle 'em. Pull 'em out by the root. Poison 'em. Burn 'em with an acetylene torch. Get a restraining order against 'em. Call in the Marines. Nuke 'em. Whatever ya gotta do . . . just kill 'em. Either that, or sell your house and move outta state.

Pinching Crustacea

One of the many seaside bottomfeeder blooms usually found growin' wild under wharf bollards. Oozes green sap and sheds.

THREATEN IT WITH DRAWN BUTTER AND SMACK IT WITH A MALLET.

Chrysanttermoose

This long-stemmed, hunchin' brown flower is some ugly! It grows in cedar swamps or near salt-covered roads.

DON'T FRET TOO MUCH ABOUT THIS ONE. THEY EVENTUALLY UPROOT AND THROW THEMSELVES AT ONCOMIN' VEHICLES.

Spleeny Anemone

Pale, anemic, high-maintenance butter-cups that only grow on manicured lawns. Will reject tap water, but thrive on the bottled kind, especially Poland Spring.

THIS ONE'S SO EASY TO KILL, IT DOESN'T SEEM SPORTIN'.

Flannelwood

This one here's a hardy river weed with a musky odor. Tends to burrow into trees. And I'll be danged if its flower ain't . . . plaid.

SURROUND IT WITH SAWDUST TILL IT GETS LUMBERLUNG.

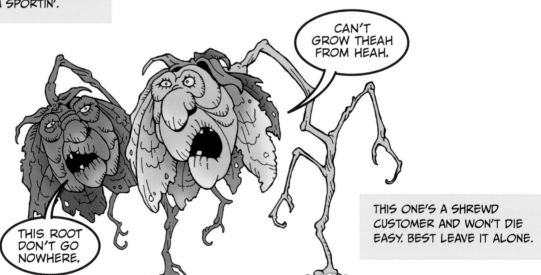

CAN'T GROW THEAH FROM HEAH.

THIS ROOT DON'T GO NOWHERE.

THIS ONE'S A SHREWD CUSTOMER AND WON'T DIE EASY. BEST LEAVE IT ALONE.

Crabby Misdirectum

These here usually crop up at out-of-the-way mom 'n' pop stores. They're crusty ol' weeds and they may look near dead, but they're about as cantankerous as a deer tick. Blooms durin' the tourist season.

PINE TREES

Eastern White Pine

This pine is the most common variety found in Maine. But it sure doesn't act common. Truth is, it's an uppity, prideful ol' thing. It'll reject your Christmas decorations if it feels they're too tacky for its high and mighty limbs. Doesn't much care for other varieties of "lesser" trees either. Some claim the first white pine came over on the *Mayflower*; maybe that explains why it acts too big for its branches.

Scotch Pine
Keeps animals up all night making bagpipe noises.

Lonesome Pine
No one'll friend them on Facebook.

STUMPER

Which of the following accessories
do not belong on a conifer?

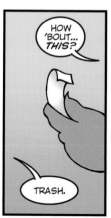

Snapshots from Maine.

I GOTTA GO, LITTLE BUDDY.

BUT I'LL SEE YOU SOON.

BYE-BYE, DADDY.

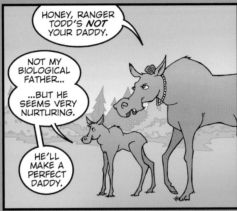

HONEY, RANGER TODD'S *NOT* YOUR DADDY.

NOT MY BIOLOGICAL FATHER...

...BUT HE SEEMS VERY NURTURING.

HE'LL MAKE A PERFECT DADDY.

JUNIOR, HE'S NOT EVEN A MOOSE.

SO? I'M NOT PREJUDICED.

YOU NEED TO LEARN THE WAYS OF THE MOOSE, JUNIOR.

YOU NEED TO KNOW WHERE TO FIND FOOD AND HOW TO DEFEND YOURSELF.

STUFF I CAN'T HELP YOU WITH.

WHAT AM I EATING?

PEANUT BUTTER AND JELLY.

IS IT MOOSE FOOD?

UH, NO.

THIS BUILDING WE'RE IN...IS IT SAFE FROM PREDATORS?

YEAH.

THAT'S WHAT I THOUGHT.

I'M STICKING WITH *YOU*.

ONCE A YEAR, BULLS USE THEIR ANTLERS TO FIGHT EACH OTHER.

IT'S CALLED RUTTING.

GREAT. ANTLERS INDUCE SOCIOPATHIC BEHAVIOR.

THAT'S JUST *PERFECT.*

YEAH, BUT THE WINNER GETS ACCESS TO THE FEMALES.

SHEESH!

AND I THOUGHT HOCKEY WAS UNCIVILIZED.

Say what?

SHORE DINNER This isn't just a meal, it's a grand buffet consisting of chowder, clams, lobster, corn on the cob, the key to the city, staff trained in CPR, and your waitress's phone number. But don't forget to leave room for the blueberry pie.

Maine Cuisine

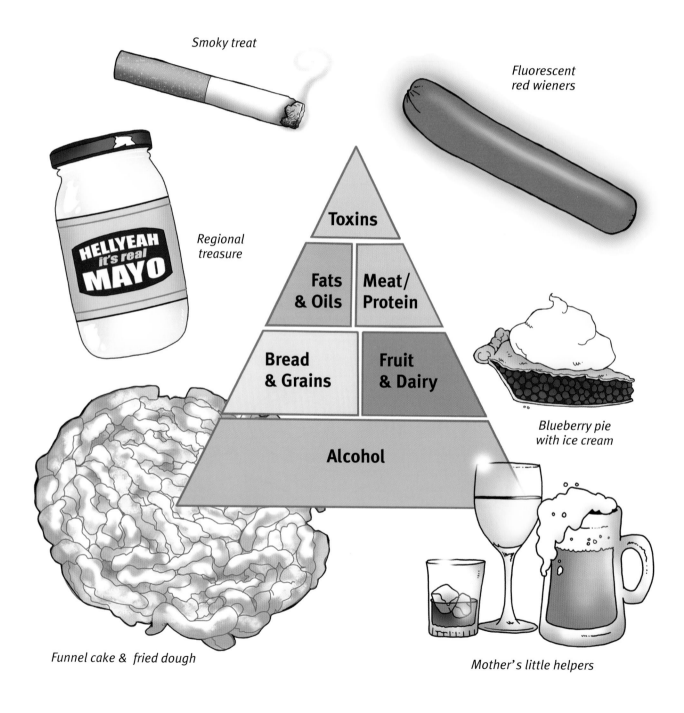

THE MAINE FOOD PYRAMID

Smoky treat

Fluorescent red wieners

Regional treasure

Toxins

Fats & Oils

Meat/ Protein

Bread & Grains

Fruit & Dairy

Alcohol

Blueberry pie with ice cream

Funnel cake & fried dough

Mother's little helpers

POTATOES

3 reasons
Maine potatoes
are some ol' good!

1 The Vitamin C in potatoes can prevent scurvy.

Scurvy Pirate

Healthy Pirate

2 Potatoes boiled in red hot dog water provide nutrition for growing babies and the dentally challenged.

HIC!

3 Distilled potato juice has been known to calm small, nervous, yapping, bug-eyed, sweater-wearing dogs.

THE MAINE COURSE: LOBSTER

*M*y grandfather met Abraham Lincoln and his wife way back when he was head cook up to Vice President Hamlin's Bangor mansion. The first family had come to visit, and it was Grandfather's job to figure out what to serve 'em for suppah. He chose lobster so's to give 'em a taste of authentic New England cookin'. In fact, he told the vice president that, for fun, he should have his honored guests drop by the kitchen. Thought they might like to pick out their own lobster. And just to give 'em an extra thrill, he suggested they should stick 'round and see how those suckers got cooked.

Well, the vice president was keen to show his guests a good time, and he for sure wanted 'em to take in the local color, so he agreed that'd be a fine idea. It didn't quite turn out the way they planned, though, because when Mrs. Lincoln caught sight of those caged and skitterin' critters, with their snappin' pinchers and beady little black eyes, she went t' twitchin'.

When Grandfather dropped one of 'em in boilin' water, and it turned red as the devil, well, Mrs. Lincoln had herself a conniption fit. She got to screamin' so much, the president had to wrassle her down.

Years later, the vice president told my grandfather that after that day, Mrs. Lincoln completely lost her mind. My grandfather thought on it a mite, looked the vice president in the eyes, and replied, "Guess I shoulda served clams."

—Earl Hornswaggle

You'll find RED, wise-cracking cartoon lobsters on T-shirts and postcards in gift shops throughout Maine. But a real lobster doesn't turn red until it hits hot water. Once that happens, they're highly unlikely to come back with an amusing bon mot.

PEOPLE TRAVEL FROM ALL OVER THE WORLD TO VISIT MAINE AND DINE ON FRESH LOBSTER. BUT VISITORS SHOULD BE WARNED TO AVOID TOURIST TRAPS...

TOURIST TRAP NEXT EXIT

...BECAUSE THE LOBSTER IS A VENGEFUL CRUSTACEAN.

HOW WOULD *YOU* LIKE IT IF I CRACKED OPEN YOUR HYBRID AND DIPPED *YOU* IN MELTED BUTTER?

How To Eat Lobster
by Earl Hornswaggle

Maine lobstah is the finest kind. Its meat is tender and sweet. But gettin' at it can be a struggle. Remembah, before you dive in, poke it a couple times. If it skitters off your plate, it ain't done. Just 'cause a bug's got a red shell, that don't make it suppah time. Lobstahs are like possums, see. When one them's fearin' danger, they'll flop over on their back, raise their legs to the sky, and play dead. Lucky for you, most of 'em are terrible actahs. However, those what've studied the Stanislavsky method have been known to hack up tomalley just to make you think they're sickly. Don't be fooled, though. Quickly toss those rascals back in the steamah, strap on yuh bib, and prepare for a treat.

WHO'LL PROVIDE FOR MY WIFE AND KIDS?

WARNING!!

THIS NEXT PART AIN'T FOR THE SQUEAMISH. FACT, IT'S JUST THE KINDA THING'LL GIVE YOUR LITTLE ONES NIGHTMARES.

TWIST! *off the claws.*

SNAP! *the flippahs off the tail.*

BREAK! *the tail from the body.*

CRACK! *open each claw.*

Lobster Fact

SOME SHELLS ARE HARDER THAN OTHERS. BUT IF YOU'RE HUNGRY ENOUGH, YOU'LL FIND A WAY TO RELEASE THE DELICIOUS MEAT TRAPPED INSIDE.

Sure, it takes a bit of effort. Heck yeah, it's messy. But let me tell you, once you get done, the eatin' is some ol' good.

RESTAURANTS

*M*aine is famous for its restaurants, lobster pounds, diners, and clam shacks. You may not find a parking spot, but the grub is usually pretty darn good. However, there are a few eateries in the Pine Tree State that just aren't up to snuff. You'd get a better meal licking the gurry off a fishing boat. Here's just a few you might want to steer clear of.

Cheap Pete's

BYOC (bring your own condiments) and prepare to sit on the concrete floor. Known for its large portions of breaded, deep-fried everything, served in heavy-duty, grease-resistant paper buckets. You won't like the taste, but you can't beat the price.

Tomalley Jack's

Every dish served looks exactly like the faded color photos on their fingerprint-smeared laminated menu. Expect acid reflux and vivid nightmares.

Beauf Bistro

Blasé, patchouli-scented vegans serve up half portions of overly garnished *je ne sais quoi* at twice the price.

P. P. Bladderbusters

Drinks are free. And the line to the unisex bathroom is long.

Briny Bob's Seafood Shanty

Of course it smells fishy. But everything on the menu is swimming in a salty, gelatinous liquid, so you know it's safe to eat.

FIDDLEHEADS

What the Elite Eat!

You know, in some places, the fiddlehead is considered the red-haired stepchild of the vegetable family. Why, some folks act like the fiddlehead's not sophisticated enough to sit alongside the all-too-refined asparagus or your snootier variety of lettuce, such as the regal romaine. Fiddleheads get treated with even less respect than some of your working-class leafy vegetables like collard, turnip, or mustard greens.

If vegetation had to go to grammar school, you know the fiddleheads would be the ones bullied out on the schoolyard. They'd get Indian burns, nipple cripples, wet willies, noogies, wedgies, and they'd most likely be pantsed. However, just like a high school geek might transform into a billion-dollar software architect, the fiddlehead, under proper supervision, can be transformed into a culinary delicacy.

CLAMBAKES

BLUEBERRY PIE

Blueberries for Sal

Good ol' Sal, she sure loves those blueberries! If a bear came between her and her favorite fruit, she'd wrestle him for them. And to keep her at her fighting weight, she prefers them cooked in deep-fried dough filled with pure cream, sour cream, cream cheese, creamery butter, a pinch of Bakewell Cream, a half-pound of sugar, and topped with bacon strips dragged through powdered sugar.

BEAN SUPPERS

The Simmer of Love

Maine is the center of a social phenomenon unlike any other—the bean supper. Drawn to the sweet, intoxicating incense of molasses and salt pork, flower children, lumberjacks, lobstermen, tourists, pirates, potato farmers, rusticators, sea-siders, and transplants of varying races and creeds come together as one in a celebration of peace, love, charity . . . and baked beans!

When I tell you it's a GAS, I'm mostly talking about the aftereffects of too much bean consumption. However, if you want to tune in, and turn on to a groovy scene, then you've got to join the legume revolution. Just remember . . . don't Bogart the potato salad.

And give yellow-eye peas a chance!

EXTRA CREDIT

HELP THIS LOBSTER FIND HIS DESTINY...

A
B
C
D

HOT TUB

THIS SPACE RESERVED

PERISHABLE RUSH! RUSH! INSULATED

PERISHABLE RUSH! RUSH! INSULATED

VACANCY

FREQUENTLY ASKED FLATLANDER QUESTION #324:

What's a Red Snapper?

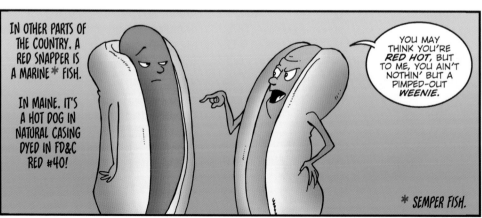

IN OTHER PARTS OF THE COUNTRY, A *RED SNAPPER* IS A MARINE * FISH.

IN MAINE, IT'S A HOT DOG IN NATURAL CASING DYED IN FD&C RED #40!

YOU MAY THINK YOU'RE *RED HOT*, BUT TO ME, YOU AIN'T NOTHIN' BUT A PIMPED-OUT *WEENIE.*

* SEMPER FISH.

Snapshots from Maine.

IT'S ANOTHER *GLORIOUS* DAY IN MAINE!

A PERFECT TIME FOR VISITORS TO COMMUNE WITH NATURE.

IT'S A BEAUTIFUL THING.

FOLKS ARE COMMUNING ALL RIGHT.

BUT MOSTLY WITH SMARTPHONES, IPADS, AND LAPTOPS.

SQUIRRELS DON'T EXACTLY *NEED* TO WEAR CLOTHES, SO WHY DO *YOU*?

MOSTLY T' IMPRESS THA LADIES.

WHY IS IT YOU WEAH CLOTHES, RANGAH TODD?

WELL, I DON'T HAVE *FUR*, SO I NEED SOME KINDA PROTECTION FROM THE ELEMENTS.

I'LL *BE*. ALL THIS TIME I THOUGHT IT WAS 'CAUSE YA WUH ASHAMED OF YUH BODY.

GIRLS! RANGER TODD HAS AGREED TO TELL US A CAMPFIRE STORY THIS EVENING.

HERE'S A REAL *DILLY* OF A TALE THAT'S BOTH INTERESTING *AND* EDUCATIONAL.

THERE *BETTER* BE A MANIAC WITH A HOOK IN THIS STORY OR I'M GOING BACK TO MY TENT.

Say what?

CAMP A Mainer's summer vacation house. It's usually found near freshwater or in the woods, but located no more than an hour from the owner's permanent residence. It's where Vacationlanders vacation. Unfortunately, most of these dwellings are darn near impossible to reach in the wintertime.

Activities & Entertainment

LIGHTHOUSE TOURS

*B*ack in the late 1700s, the inhabitants of Seguin Island were vehemently opposed to the erection of Maine's very first lighthouse. They believed the towering monstrosity would ruin the view. But with all the ships banging into each other out in the fog, they were forced to build it anyway. In time, ships would be equipped with their own lights and radar. Once that happened, many islanders considered tearing down that old eyesore. As fate would have it, a few business-minded visionaries came up with a better idea—turn the lighthouse into a tourist attraction. To this very day, vacationers from all over the world flock in droves just to visit that old relic.

Famous Lighthouses

Portland Head Light

West Quoddy Head Light

Bass Harbor Head Light

Norumbega Trailer Park Light

SUMMER SPORTS

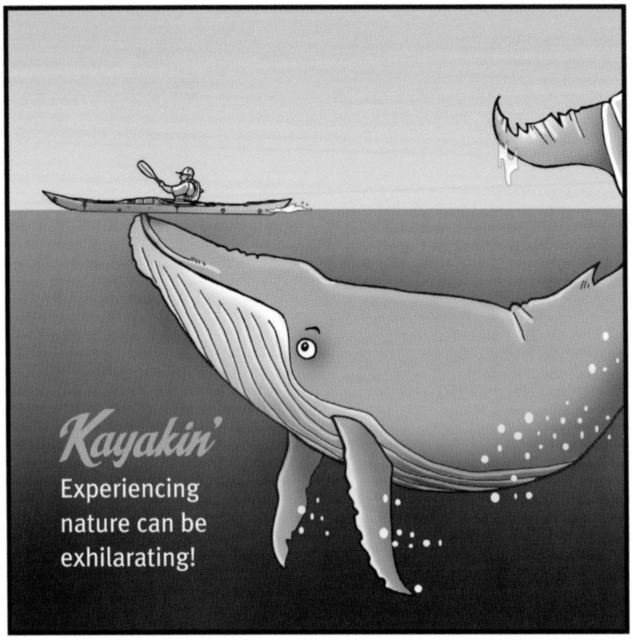
Kayakin'
Experiencing nature can be exhilarating!

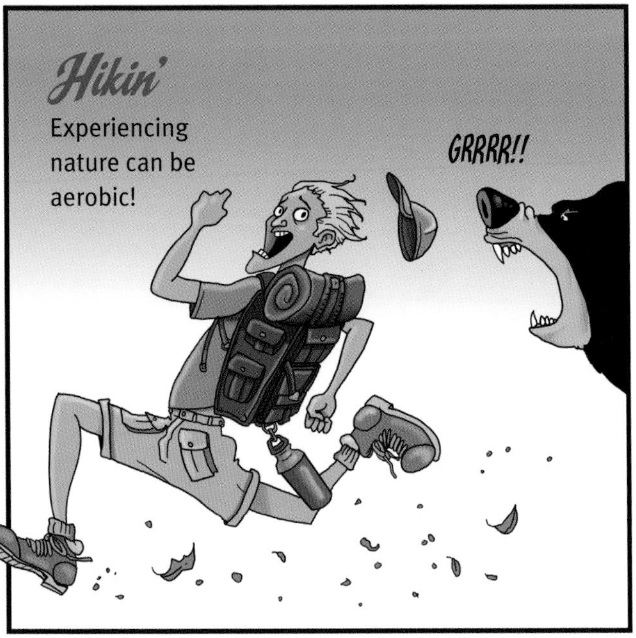
Hikin'
Experiencing nature can be aerobic!
GRRRR!!

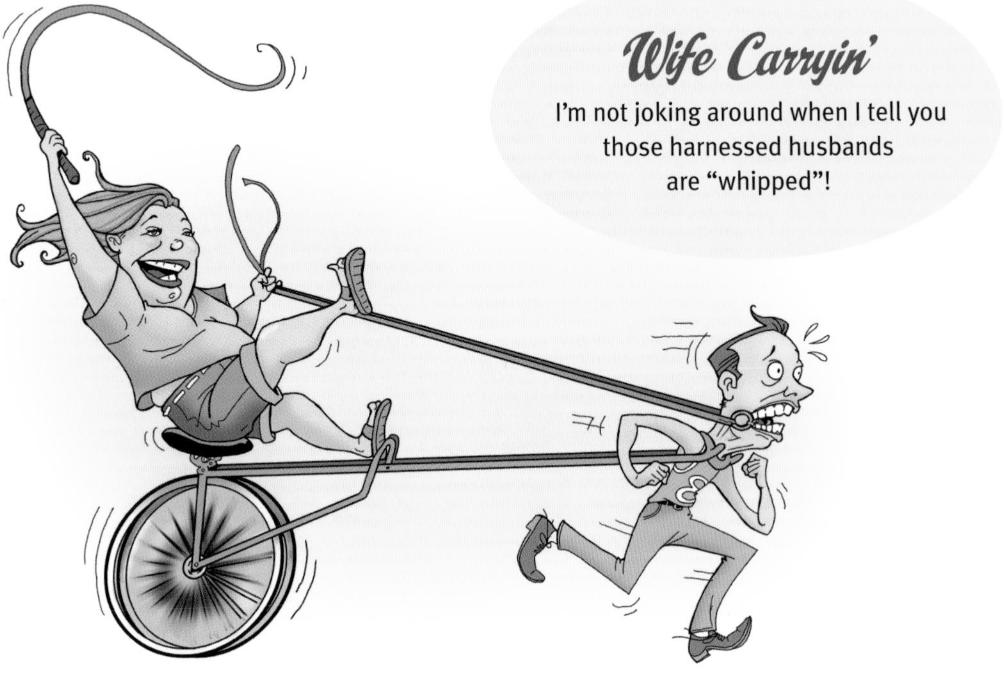
Wife Carryin'
I'm not joking around when I tell you those harnessed husbands are "whipped"!

Fishin'

Folks come from all over the world to drop a fishing line in Maine waters. But fancy tackle won't make you a fisherman. You've got to prepare if you want to reel in these local rascals. Every fish found in Maine has its own fighting style. And some of 'em fight as ugly as they look.

WINTER SPORTS

Ice Fishin'

If getting smashed was a sport, this would be the perfect winter event.

Sleddin'

Not much difference between a bobsled and a vehicle with bald tires.

Ice Skatin'

Some days getting from your vehicle to your house requires the skills of a competitive figure skater.

Dog Sleddin'

S'just foolish.

Driveway Shovelin'

The game is on! Competitors race to clear the end of their drive before the city snowplow adds to the pile.

TREASURE HUNT

ARRR! Thar be treasures beyond yer wildest dreams hidden deep within the bowels of Maine.
Set sail to the Pine Tree State, me hearties, and claim yer PRIZE!

A. L.L. Bean Store

B. Marden's Dumpster

C. Yard Sale

D. Transfer Station (Dump)

Snapshots from Maine.

FIRST THING I WANNA *SEE*—ONE THOSE GORGEOUS LIGHTHOUSES. HOW 'BOUT *YOU*, ANGIE?

WHEN I'M LOST INNA SNOW STORM, SURROUNDED BY WOLVES, MAYBE *DEN* YOU'LL WISH WE NEVER LEFT JERSEY.

GEEZ, *VITO*, AIN'T YA GONNA SAY SOMETHIN'? YOUR DAUGHTER'S TALKIN' *CRAZY* OVER HERE.

AIN'T NO MORE WOLVES IN MAINE, SWEETHEART. *BUT* DEY DO GOT COYOTES.

FELLA IN THE CAR THEY-AH'S CARTIN' OUTTA STATE SQUIRRELS UP TO THE PAHK.

S'POSE HE ASKED FAH DIRECTIONS?

AYUH, AN' HE WAS RIGHT TICKLED WHEN I SAID "YOU CAN'T GET THEY-AH FROM HEAH."

ONE THESE DAYS I'M GONNA GIVE OUT *PROPAH* DIRECTIONS TO A TOURIST.

DON'T CARE *HOW* MUCH IT DISAPPOINTS 'EM.

NEW SQUIRREL FAMILY WANTS T' MOVE IN, EH?

THEY'RE FROM NEW JERSEY.

WELL SIR, THIS HEAH GROVE'S LIKE ONE THOSE FANCY *GATED* COMMUNITIES.

RESIDENTS *VOTE* ON WHO GETS TO LIVE HEAH.

NO FLATLANDAHS!

POK!

AND THEY-AH'S *ONE* VOTE COUNTED.

Say what?

WILLIWAWS An uncomfortable feeling. Like the one you might get on the Tilt-A-Whirl at Old Orchard Beach after making a meal of cotton candy and fried dough. Or the one you might get once you realize that Stephen King's Maine is not actually the stuff of fiction. That's right, your nightmares are real!

Legends

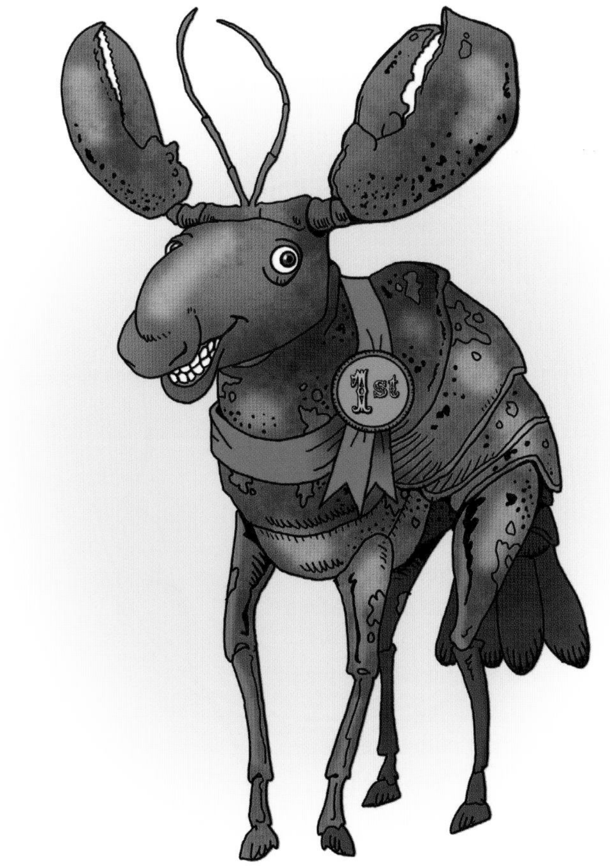
1st

PAULIE BUNIONS

*T*hose tales 'bout Paul Bunyan, 'bout him bein' this huge bear-of-a-man that could clear a thicket with one ax swing— they're all a load o' hooey. See, Paul was a squirrelly little hunch-back. His eyesight was so bad, the lenses on his glasses were thick as the bottom of a Moxie bottle. I think Jean-Paul Bouillabaisse mighta been his real name. Somethin' French like that. Up to camp, we all called him Paulie "Bunions" on account of his swollen toes. They were so big, he had to wear special-made boots that ballooned up the toe—looked like clown shoes.

Paulie Bunions was, without a doubt, the worst lumberjack ever lived. Ya see, that's why the boys up to camp used to spin wild yarns 'bout him. It was s'pose to be funny. The jokes were ironical, like when you name a fat boy "Slim." 'Cause Paulie, well, he wunt no lumberjack. That's for certain. Point of fact, he was the camp mascot. The more superstitious drivers used to rub his head for luck every mornin' afore they headed out to work.

Don't get me wrong—Paulie was more'n just a good luck charm; he was the heart and soul of the camp.

Everybody loved him, especially the camp cookee, Miss Babe. Time was, all that ol' girl cared about was eatin' her weight in beans and biscuits. Then Babe caught sight o' Paulie. She looked at Paulie as if he were a stack o' doughnuts. Ol' Babe was big as an ox and stronger'n a bull moose, but she'd stutter and turn butter-legged whenever Paulie'd come to the cookshack. Paulie was pretty smitten with her too, and it wunt 'cause his eyesight was poorly. Paulie knew that come the teeth-chatterin' cold o' winter, a gal of her girth made for better cuddlin' than a bluetick hound. She was a skinny man's dream come true, all right, so he up and proposed afore first frost.

Babe and Paulie's weddin' was one heckuva shindig. The whole camp smelled o' rose water, fried smelt and woodsmoke. Doc Sawbones played the weddin' march on his squeezebox and the bride come out lookin' like a shimmerin' white tent trimmed in lace. Paulie, standin' by the preacher, smilin' ear to ear, musta thought himself the luckiest man alive. He stood so proud, you could barely see his hunch. Damned if it didn't seem like he grew an inch when the preacher asked if Paulie'd take Babe to be his lawfully wedded wife. Well sir, ol' Paulie was just about to say his "I do's" when the drive boss yelled out, "LOG JAM!" Quick as rabbits, the weddin' party took off runnin'. Paulie, quite naturally, followed after 'em, leavin' his poor bride-to-be all alone and fumin' at the altar.

Now, Babe, she had a hair-trigger temper, and Paulie runnin' off like that was just the sort of thing to set her off. You know how a blue flame is hotter 'n red one? Well, when steam come pourin' out her nostrils, her pinched face turned more'n a few shades of blue. But who could blame her, this was s'posed to be the happiest time of her life. And, wouldn't you know it, just when that poor girl thought her big day couldn't get no worse, the drive boss called out, "MAN DOWN!"

It was Paulie. He wunt even s'posed to be out there ridin' logs, but he got all caught up in the excitement. Once he started in jabbin' at the jam with a pick pole, he lost his balance, rolled a bit, then up and fell in. Well, Babe, seein' her man was in danger, didn't waste no time. She hiked up her gown and jumped in after him. Darn near drained the river on impact, partin' water like Moses himself. Bound and determined to rescue her true love, she pushed logs aside like they were naught but toothpicks. She even cleared the jam. After that, and not a minute too soon, Babe hauled her near-drowned sweetheart up to the shore and brought him back with the kiss o' life. Then Babe looked Paulie straight in the eyes, wagged a finger at him, and says, "You're not gonna get outta marryin' me that easy, Mister Man."

—Earl Hornswaggle

INFERNAL COMBUSTION

The scariest Halloween I recollect was in 1970, back in the day when I owned a service station up to Veazie, Earl's Gas and Grease. It was a good ol' shop, one of those full-service jobbies with gas pumps, a coke-cola machine, and a mechanic on duty. Anyway, that Halloween, just after dark, a kid named Steve from up the university brought his car in to be fixed. She was a beauty—a 1958 white-over-red two-toned finned Plymouth Fury. Purred like a pampered house cat. Looked mint. But, according to young Steve, it had a few problems. "She sometimes switches on all by herself," he said. "It's like she's got a mind of her own."

Olie, my mechanic, cracked a smile, figurin' the kid was pullin' some kinda Halloween prank. But that boy was dead serious. "This may sound crazy," he said, "but one time, when my girlfriend Tabby was waiting for

me at the Oronoka parking lot, the car doors locked—all by themselves."

Olie didn't believe a word of it, but he told Steve he'd give the car a good goin' over. So Steve left the Fury in Olie's hands and took off in a town cab.

Olie drove her into the bay and looked under the hood. He listened to the motor. He fiddled with the wires. He even rolled underneath to check the oil pan. But I'll be darned if he couldn't find one blessed thing wrong with that car. So Olie did what any frustrated mechanic might do—he kicked one of the tires, hard as he could, with his steel-toed boot.

Well sir, I'll tell you what, that car didn't much care for bein' kicked. She made a terrible noise, like a wounded bull moose. Then there come a flash o' sparks just afore the garage lights knocked out. But we weren't in the dark for long, cause the Fury's headlights flashed on bright enough to blind a man. Olie and I backed up against the garage wall, petrified. 'Bout that time, the Fury's radio switched on and started in playin' some ground-shakin', pulse-poundin' devil music. Olie and I just stood there, frozen in place, watchin' that car rock, roll, and flop to the beat like a fish on dry land. Then that Fury stood up on her hind tires, roared, fell back on all fours, and I swear I saw her grill form the shape of a smile. Once she got settled down, Olie took to his heels. He flew from out that garage like a man on fire, never to show hide nor hair ever again.

Next day, the kid, Steve, come back to the station, hopin' to hear some good news. But when I told him we couldn't find nothin' wrong with his car, that boy gave a look like he was visitin' the family dog up the pet cemetery. Just 'bout broke my heart. So I give him a little somethin' to go on. "There is this one needful thing," I said. "Her tires are extremely sensitive. You might want t' look into replacin' 'em."

—*Earl Hornswaggle*

MARIE ANTOINETTE'S CATS

JUST WATCHED A DOCUMENTARY ABOUT THE FRENCH REVOLUTION.

THEY EVEN MENTIONED *MAINE* IN IT.

DID YOU KNOW THAT THE QUEEN OF FRANCE, MARIE ANTOINETTE, TRIED TO ESCAPE HER ENEMIES BY FLEEING TO AMERICA? TO WISCASSET, MAINE, OF ALL PLACES.

DIDN'T SHE GET EXECUTED?

1791

"*SURE*, BUT A WHOLE BUNCH OF MARIE ANTOINETTE'S PRIZED POSSESSIONS WOUND UP SAILING TO MAINE WITHOUT HER.

ONCE WE REACH MAINE, WE'LL RAISE AN ARMY.

ZEN WE'LL RETURN TO FRANCE AND *TAKE BACK* ZE THRONE!

"AMONG THEM... HER THREE PAMPERED CATS!"

WE'LL MAKE ZOZE FEEL-TY PEASANTS EAT *CROW!*

I SOT WE WANTED ZEM TO EAT CAKE?

Therese.

Coco.

Sophie.

CREATURES OF LEGEND

Lunksoos

That's the Wabanaki name for a particularly vicious wildcat also known as the Indian devil. It's said that this prehistoric saber-toothed cat was once frozen at the bottom of the Lunksoos Lake, but thawed out sometime in the 1800s. If you woke up in the middle of a lake after a 9,000-year nap, wouldn't you be cranky?

PocoMoonshine Monster

He's huge, awkward, bashful, and being the only one of his kind has made him a bit self-conscious. He's pretty jittery, too. Especially when folks point at him and scream in terror.

SQUEAL!

The Maine Monster

The menacing left-field wall at Portland's Hadlock Field.

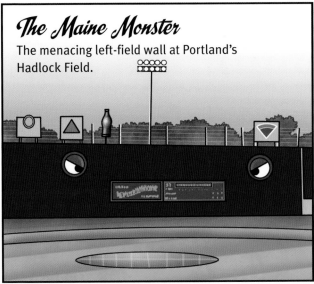

Billdad

A small creature, about ankle-high, that makes a noise that sounds as if it's saying the word "wazzat." Anybody who ventures into the Maine woods searching for a Billdad has probably had too much to drink. Those who find one are most definitely over the legal limit.

WAZZAT!

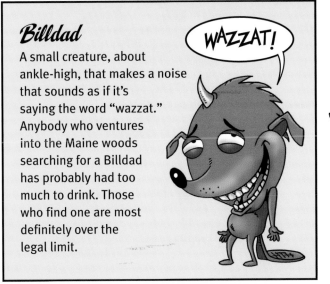

The Rat Pack

A clique of celebrated bull moose known for their wild partying and roguish seduction of cows.

Frank

Sammy

Dino

STUMPER

Which of the following folkloric beasties, according to Abenaki mythology, is said to be the protector of Mount Katahdin?

Timber Belle Fairy

Bean Bug

Pennywise Spider

Pamola

Snapshots from Maine.

TWO BULLS IN THE HEAT OF RUTTING SEASON BATTLE FOR SUPERIORITY, LIKE KNIGHTS OF OLD, IN AN ANTLER-CLASHING JOUST...

ARGH!

GRR!

...SO THAT THE CHAMPION MIGHT WIN A FAIR DAMSEL'S HOOF AND HEART!

KA-CHUNK!

THAT'S *GOTTA* HURT.

BEING A BACHELOR'S NOT SOUNDING HALF-BAD.

SOUND? WHAT SOUND? ALL I CAN HEAR IS THE BIRDIES.

TWEET TWEET TWEET TWEET TWEET TWEET

AT THE END OF EVERY RUTTING MATCH THE WINNING BULL RECEIVES A YEAR'S SUPPLY OF SALT LICK, A FULLY STOCKED COW HAREM AND THE ADMIRATION OF ALL HIS PEERS.

HOWEVER, THE LOSER USUALLY WINDS UP WITH BRAIN DAMAGE, A STUTTER, A CRACKED RACK, AND AN UNCONTROLLABLE FACIAL TICK.

YES, NATURE CAN BE CRUEL.

TOP OF THE WORLD, MA! TOP OF THE WORLD!

C-COULDA BUH-BEEN A CA-CONTEND-DAH, INSTEAD OF A BUH-BUH-BUM... WHICH IS W-WHAT I Y-YAM.

UHM, I KNOW I SHOULDN'T BE ATTRACTED TO YOU, BUT...

DUH-DON'T TRY T-TO CH-CHANGE ME, BUH-BABY.

I LOST MY HUSBAND IN THE STORM. CAN YOU HELP ME FIND HIM?

THAT'S MY JOB, MA'AM.

HE'S 10 FT. LONG, 6 FT. HIGH, WEIGHS 1200 LBS, AND HE'S SHEDDING HIS ANTLERS.

SO, UH, HE'S LIKE AN *AVERAGE* BULL MOOSE, THEN?

WELL, HE MAY NOT BE *SPECIAL*, BUT...

...I STILL WANT HIM BACK.

Say what?

YARD SALE An informal event for the sale of used goods, usually held in a Mainer's dooryard (front yard). Unwanted Christmas gifts are popular resale items. Well, popular with everyone except those who gave the gift in the first place. You're also likely to find exercise bikes, workout tapes, and weights for sale. Barely used, but they may emit the smell of good intention.

Shopping

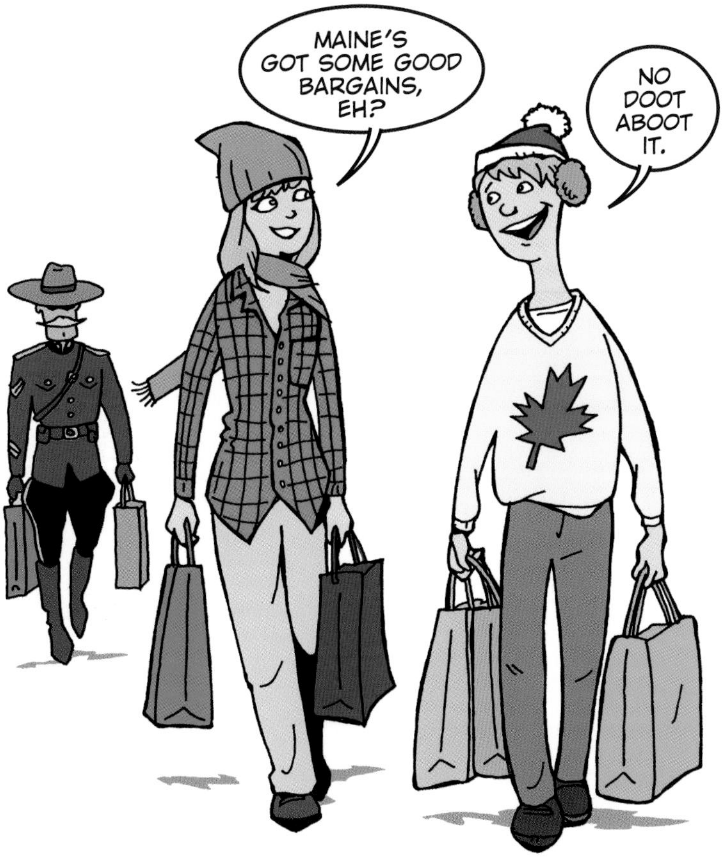
MAINE'S GOT SOME GOOD BARGAINS, EH?
NO DOOT ABOOT IT.

SOUVENIRS

*Y*ou wouldn't drop by Disneyland without coming home with one those silly hats with the mouse ears, would you? Heck no! So don't leave Maine without picking up some of these "wicked good" trinkets, found at fine tourist traps from Kittery to Madawaska.

Not just a look, it's a lifestyle.

Tourists find this keychain funny.
Most Mainers find it practical.

With this shirt, you can share your love of Maine AND your love of self.

This is Vacationland. Even the police stations have gift shops.

Can't say I understand fashion, but this buoy necklace could be helpful if you're not much of a swimmer.

Blackfly welts—they're free. Take home as many as you want.

Not the best reminder of your vacation, but you're gonna pick up quite a few while you're here.

Mainers are trying to cut back on tobacco, but these can come in handy when it comes to tick removal.

Relive your romantic honeymoon in Maine with these seductive lobster-inspired garments.

CATALOGS

Hardscrabble Country Store

Hoarders and packrats beware! This catalog contains yard sale and flea market items repackaged and adorned with lots of pretty ribbon and a pine tree air freshener. Featured items include personalized concrete blocks used for trailer stabilization, holiday-themed decorative Bondo, and vintage long johns patched up so many times the original fabric's hardly visible. Patriotic promotional descriptions make it seem almost un-American not to place an order.

Cunnin' Creations

A collection of Maine-themed items so cutesy-wutesy, they are, at first, irresistible. Catalog features a warehouse full of cheesy novelty products guaranteed to incite ridicule and public mocking.

PRICED TO MOVE
HOKEY CERAMIC STATUETTES OF SMALL, WIDE-EYED CHILDREN DRESSED LIKE LOBSTER-MEN, LUMBERJACKS, TOURISTS, AND HOMESTEAD HIPPIES.

Splinter Gallery

The catalog that claims anything carved out of wood with a chain saw should be considered ART is back! Items include the bobbing-head woodland creatures collection. Plus, you'll find a large array of decorative chain saws. Airbrushed designs include the popular silhouette of a naked lady or the flame-spitting skull. Smaller, feminine models available in floral and pink plaid.

Rascal Outlet

Nothing passes the time quite like reckless behavior, an inappropriate use of explosives, and running with a sharp object. The Rascal Outlet catalog offers everything from flamethrowers, switchblades, and gelignite to those ATVs designed with your bratty, prepubescent daredevil in mind. If there's a felon, arsonist, and/or delinquent on your gift list, this is the catalog for you.

LET THE WILD RUCKUS START!

Thank You for Visiting!

The best way to understand Maine is to experience it. I recommend you pack a bag or two and do some exploring on your own. I don't have any ties to the Maine Board of Tourism, but I think they're right when they boast that life in Maine is the way life should be. Don't take my word for it, though; come find out for yourself. And if you're just coming for a visit, you'll want to take as many of my books as possible back home with you. How else are you going to share your adventure with friends and family? You're welcome.

—*Mark Scott Ricketts*

Over the years, Maine's beautiful landscape has inspired many artists, writers, and outdoor enthusiasts. Unfortunately, the animals around here are chatty and obnoxious. But, hey, as long as you don't feed them, they'll probably leave you alone. Eventually.

—*Ranger Todd*

Maine is for Mainers; everybody else get out!

—*Earl Hornswaggle*

The views expressed in this book are not necessarily those of the Maine Board of Tourism.

Glossary

CHUMMY: If a Mainer refers to you in this manner, he's probably not being cordial.

CUNNIN': Cute. Like a baby, or a litter of kittens before you realize they're feral.

DEE-AH (sp. "dear"): A salutation much like the word "chummy," which can be used with either endearment or scorn.

DOWN EAST: Some folks will tell you it's the old coastal sailing route from Boston to Nova Scotia. Some folks will tell you it's a state of mind.

FINEST KIND: It's all good. The tip-toppity.

FLATLANDER: If you don't know by now, you're probably one.

FROM AWAY: Mainers describe flatlanders in a variety of ways. This one's pretty darn tame.

GURRY: Fish entrails, especially those that adhere to your boat. To be "all gurried up" is to be slathered with fish guts.

MINGE: A tiny, annoying insect.

MUCKLE: If a moose is barreling toward your vehicle and a Mainer uses this word, you better grab hold of something and hang on.

RUSTICATOR: A summer visitor, usually one who stays for the entire summer. I'm told that those who spend too much time near the water will oxidize and turn a reddish color.

SHEDDER: A molting lobster. Also known as soft-shell lobster. While cheaper in price than hard-shell lobster, some may argue that they're past their prime.

SUMMER COMPLAINT: A tourist, a flatlander, a wallet with legs, and an annoyance with no sense of direction.

THE COUNTY: Doesn't matter what county in Maine you live in, Aroostook is the only one that holds the distinction of being "THE" County. Aroostook seceded from the Union years ago, but has yet to inform the rest of the state. Also known as "the Potato Empire," "Spud-opolis," and "The Tuber Zone."

TOMALLEY: (Not to be confused with "Tamale") It's the digestive gland of a lobster. It turns green when cooked. Some consider it a delicacy, but I've seen others turn green after eating it.

TOTE ROAD: A private dirt road that burrows through the woods and is usually used for hauling stuff in and out. If you're writing a manifesto, you'll likely take one to get to your shotgun shack.

TRANSPLANT: A flatlander who has taken up residence in Maine.

UGLY: If you're so cranky that a Mainer calls you this, you may want to check your blood sugar.

UNCLE HENRY'S CLASSIFIEDS: A weekly reminder of the accessibility of stuff you really don't need.

CERTIFICATE OF GRADUATION

THIS CERTIFIES THAT

· ·

HAS WITH OUTSTANDING ACHIEVEMENT
SATISFACTORILY PARTICIPATED IN AND
SUCCESSFULLY COMPLETED A COURSE IN

MAINE STUDIES

AND IS THEREFORE ENTITLED TO THE RIGHTS
AND PRIVILEGES APPERTAINING THERETO

Mark Scott Ricketts

IS A MAINE-BASED WRITER AND ILLUSTRATOR WHO'S WORKED WITH *PLAYBOY* MAGAZINE, MCGRAW HILL, DARK HORSE COMICS, *NICKELODEON* MAGAZINE, AND MORE. AMONG OTHER PROJECTS, HE WROTE *IRON MAN: THE SINGULARITY (AVENGERS DISASSEMBLED)* FOR MARVEL COMICS AND *NIGHT TRIPPERS* FOR IMAGE COMICS.

THERE'S REALLY NO REASON TO MENTION THAT HE'S BEEN A SODA JERK, AN ART DIRECTOR, A SONGWRITER, A MONTHLY MAGAZINE COLUMNIST, A CARTOON CHARACTER, A WEBCOMIC CREATOR, A RACE TRACK OYSTER SHUCKER, AND A GRAVEYARD SHIFT CASHIER AT A CONVENIENCE STORE, RIGHT?